# Growing Fuchsias

# Growing Fuchsias

K. Jennings   V. Miller

CROOM HELM LONDON

© 1979 K. Jennings and V. Miller
Croom Helm Ltd, 2-10 St John's Road, London SW11

British Library Cataloguing in Publication Data

Jennings, K
    Growing fuchsias
    1. Fuchsia
    I. Title
    635.9'33'44        SB413.F8
    ISBN 0-85664-890-6

Reprinted 1980

Printed in Great Britain by Biddles Ltd, Guildford, Surrey

# Contents

# Acknowledgements

This book has resulted from the experience and enjoyment gained from close involvement over many years with fuchsias and the people who grow them.

It has been our privilege to have witnessed and indeed to have taken part in much of the work of the British Fuchsia Society, who's permission to reproduce their revised *Plant Form Definition and Judging Criteria* is gratefully acknowledged. We wish also to thank those many friends and associates who have without hestitation given freely of their advice and help, not all of which will be obvious in the finished product but which has nevertheless been instrumental to this end. In particular we are indebted to Miss E.J. Willson FLA for complete freedom to quote from her absorbing biography of James Lee and the Vineyard Nursery, Hammersmith, in which is revealed a fascinating insight of the life of James Lee and the era in which he lived. To Mr and Mrs Ewart, Mr L. Boullemier, and Mr G. Gorrod, all of the British Fuchsia Society; to Mr Carl Wallace for photographs and to Mr C.F. Jennings for the line drawings and photographs. Acknowledgements other than those mentioned within the text are given in the references to chapter 1.

# Foreword

The fuchsia with its delicate and graceful blooms has over the past decade or two regained its rightful place amongst the most popular of plants. It can be trained in ways almost legion, it flowers freely, and the number of cultivars that can be purchased for a very modest figure runs into thousands.

Fuchsias are enjoying a deserved popularity in most of the temperate countries in the world and part of the development in some small way could be attributed to the authors of this book.

Both are accredited British Fuchsia Society National Judges, well known for their skills and experience in all aspects of fuchsia culture including administration and showbench organisation at National level.

It is a privilege to write this Foreword to a book which is considered to be different to others written on the same subject. It includes almost every aspect of cultivation written in a manner so fully and clearly that few who study it would miss the right road to success.

Leo B. Boullemier

Figure 1.1
*F. magellanica
macrostemma*
(Thilco). Copy
of Feuille's
original drawing
*circa* 1725

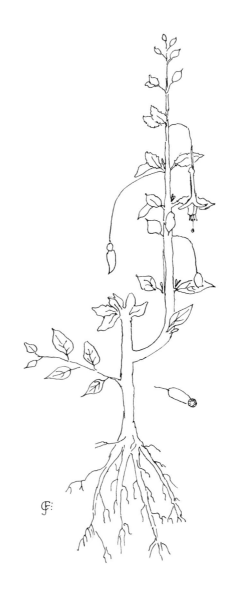

# The Fuchsia (Onagraceae)

## A Short History

The history of the fuchsia can be traced back some 275 years to 1703 with the publication of *Nova Plantarum Americanum Genera*, the work of a missionary and botanist, Father Carole Plumier. Among the many new species and genera described was one that was to become the first recorded species of the genus *Fuchsia*, named by Plumier as *Fuchsia triphylla flore coccinea*, the generic name referring to Leonhard Fuchs, a sixteenth-century botanist and doctor of medicine who held the chair of medicine at Tubingen University from 1535 until his death in 1566.

Fuchs is most remembered for his great work *De Historia Stirpium*, a Latin herbal that dealt with some 400 plants native to Germany together with about 100 other foreign plants. Even today herbalists still regard this as a standard reference work. It is thought that Plumier was greatly influenced by the writings of Fuchs and, in honouring him by naming the newly discovered genus after him there is no doubt that it was done in respect and admiration. The practice of having a plant named in one's honour was a privilege much sought after in the late eighteenth century, a time when plants were being discovered and recorded in accordance with the Linnean binomial system.

The exact location of Plumier's find was not recorded and remained something of a mystery for almost 170 years, during which time there appeared the first edition of *Species Plantarum*. Published in 1737, this was the work of the Swedish naturalist Karl von Linne, commonly called Linnaeus, who in recording Plumier's new genus based it entirely upon the original, though somewhat inexact, description given by Plumier. He also omitted the *flore coccinea* and in accordance with the rules he had laid down it appeared as *Fuchsia triphylla* only.

Later discoveries of fuchsia species were to some extent a vindication of Plumier's find, but it was not until 1873 that Thomas Hogg[1] of New York, in sending home some seed, definitely settled its existence and native location, which is variously recorded as San Domingo or Haiti. This apparently contradictory statement of where Hogg's seed actually came from deserves some explanation. The Caribbean island of Hispaniola is divided into the Dominican Republic, covering an area of nearly 20,000 square miles, and the capital of which is San Domingo (a former Spanish colony), and the Republic of Haiti, formerly a French colony covering some 11,000 square miles. The city of San Domingo was founded by a brother of Christopher Columbus, who had discovered the island in 1492.

In 1882, Hendersons,[2] a firm of nurserymen of St John's Wood, London, sent a plant to Kew for identification. This was the first plant of *F. triphylla* to be seen in this country and is thought to have been raised from the seed that Thomas Hogg had sent home to New York, as Hendersons had acquired their plants from America. At this time there would seem to have been at least two species in cultivation in this country as it is recorded that Kew had received a plant of *F. coccinea*[3] in 1788 from a Captain Firth.[4] It is around this plant that the famous story of James Lee of the Vineyard Nursery, Hammersmith, has been woven. Most historians in recounting this story give the impression that Lee was a man who was more interested in making money from his plants than he was interested in the plants themselves, and the rather wild story of him having procured a plant of *F. coccinea* from which he is purported to have propagated some 300 plants which he sold at between 10 to 20 guineas each,[5] does little for the reputation of the man who, in 1793, introduced the fuchsia to the English public.

Lee was born in Selkirkshire in 1715 and left home at the age of 17, with little more than an average education and a knowledge of Latin, to walk to London. His early life was spent in the employ of the Duke of Argyle at Whitton Place where, according to Dr Thornton (who wrote a sketch of Lee's life) the Duke 'continued his education and allowed him the free use of his library'[6]. He would also appear at some time to have worked under Phillip Miller, the author of the *Gardener's Dictionary*, who was in charge of the Apothecaries' Garden at Chelsea from 1722-69. Other famous names who worked under Miller included William Forsyth, later to become superintendent of the Royal Gardens at Kensington[7] and whose name is perpetuated by the flowering shrub Forsythia, and William Aiton of the Royal Botanic Gardens at Kew.

Aiton compiled a catalogue of plants, cultivated at Kew, which he published in 1789 as *Hortus Kewensis*. He tried to show, as far as possible, when each plant listed was first introduced into England and it was James Lee who helped with information about the trees acquired by Kew from Whitton, on the death of the Duke of Argyle in 1761.[8]

The partnership of James Lee and Lewis Kennedy in the Vineyard Nursery garden at Hammersmith commenced about 1745 and, being situated on the main road from London and, described by Bowack[9] in 1705 as an area having 'several good Houses in and about it, inhabited by Gentry and Persons of Quality and for above an hundred years past has been a summer Retreat for Nobility and Wealthy citizens . . .', seems to have been well situated for the success and fame that was to follow.

In 1761 Lee published *An Introduction to Botany* which was largely a translation of the *Philosophia Botanica* of Linnaeus and over the next 50 years was extended to ten editions. The last of these carried the previously mentioned sketch of Lee's life by Dr Robert Thornton in which he attributed two scientific observations to Lee:

> He discovered which Islands had belonged to Europe and what to Asia by the heath (Erica) which is abundantly dispersed over Europe, Africa and America; but is not found in Asia or any of its islands which once formed part of that continent . . . He generally observed, that, for want of insects to further the nuptials of plants, or a proper degree of ventilation, or rather favouring breezes, or from some defect in the escape of pollen from the anthers, that the seeds in stove plants are in general unproductive, and for a series of years artificial impregnation has been performed at Hammersmith which always secured an increase, and proves the practical value of science.

Lee also produced a pamphlet entitled 'Rules for collecting and preserving Seed from Botany Bay'. The Vineyard Nursery was the first to have seed from Botany Bay, due mainly to the great friendship of Lee with Joseph Banks, who had accompanied Captain Cook on his first voyage round the world. Botany Bay was so named because of the large number of specimens found there by Banks[10] and 'Saw-leaved Banksea'[11] was the first to be raised from seed received from there by the nursery.

Joseph Banks, later to become Sir Joseph Banks, founded the King's garden at Kew as a botanical garden. He had the cultivation of tea introduced to India from China and helped found both the Linnean Society of London and the Royal Horticultural Society. He was also president of the Royal Society for 42 years and a Trustee of the British Museum.

In April 1776 Lee recommended a young gardener, David Nelson, to Joseph Banks as suitable to act as a plant collector on Captain Cook's third voyage round the world. Nelson was successful and in

1787 Banks in turn recommended him to Lord Sandwich for a similar voyage which was intended to introduce the breadfruit tree to the West Indies. Unfortunately for Nelson the ship was the *Bounty* and its Captain was William Bligh. During the voyage the crew mutinied and Nelson was one of those set adrift and later died of exposure at Keopang (Kupang), in Indonesian Timor north-west of Darwin, Australia.[12]

Another patron of the Vineyard Nursery was Thomas Jefferson, the author of the Declaration of Independence and the third President of the United States, who had plants sent from the nursery to friends and had their catalogue of plants and seeds in his library.[13]

There is little doubt that Lee was one of the foremost and most respected botanists of his time with a very wide circle of famous friends and patrons. *Hortus Kewensis* lists 135 plants introduced into England, or first known as cultivated by the Vineyard Nursery during the lifetime of James Lee. They came from North America, south Europe, from the Alps of Germany and Italy, from Siberia, the Cape of Good Hope, Chile, Canada, Austria, Madeira, Portugal, the East Indies, Spain, New South Wales, China, the West Indies, Jamaica, Cayenne, Guinea, Sierra Leone, Greece and Mexico, mostly as seeds sent by correspondents, although they later sent out their own collectors.[14]

To most fuchsia enthusiasts James Lee is known as the man who persuaded a woman living in Wapping to part with a plant that he had seen growing on the window sill of her house and so the story goes, made a great deal of money from this piece of opportunism. This story, which appeared for the first time in the *Lincoln Herald* of 4 November 1831, is recounted here in full:

> Old Mr. Lee, a nurseryman and gardener near London, well-known fifty or sixty years ago, was one day showing his variagated treasures to a friend, who suddenly turned to him and declared, 'Well, you have not in your collection a prettier flower than I saw this morning at Wapping', 'No! and pray what is this phoenix like?' 'Why, the plant was elegant, and the flowers hung in rows like tasels from the pendent branches, their colour the richest crimson, in the centre a fold of deep purple', and so forth. Particular directions being demanded and given, Mr. Lee posted off to the place, where he saw, and at once perceived that the plant was new in this part of the world. He saw and admired. Entering the house, 'My good woman, this is a nice plant. I should like to buy it.' 'Ah, sir, I could not sell it for no money, for it was brought me from the West Indies by my husband, who has now left again and I must keep it for his sake'. But I must have it'. 'No, Sir!' 'Here' (emptying his pockets) 'here is gold,

silver and copper' — his stock was something more than eight guineas. 'Well-a-day, but this is a power of money, sure and sure'. 'Tis yours, and the plant is mine and my good dame shall have one of the first young ones I rear to keep for your husband's sake'. 'Alack, Alack!' 'You shall, I say'. A coach was called in which was safely deposited our florist and his seemingly dear purchase. His first work was to pull off and utterly destroy every vestige of blossom and blossom-bud, it was devided into cuttings which were forced into bark beds and hot beds, were redevided and sub-devided. Every effort was used to multiply the plant. By the commencement of the next flowering season Mr. Lee was the delighted possessor of three hundred fuchsia plants all giving promise of blossom. The two which opened first were removed to his show house. A lady came. 'Why Mr. Lee, my dear Mr. Lee, where did you get this charming flower?' 'Hem! 'tis a new thing my lady — pretty! 'tis lovely.' 'Its price?' ' A guinea; thank your ladyship', and one of the two plants stood proudly in her lady-ship's boudoir. 'My dear Charlotte! where did you get' etc. 'Oh!' tis a new thing that I saw at old Mr. Lee's. Pretty, is it not?' 'Pretty! tis beautiful! Its price?' 'A guinea; there is another left'. The visitor's horses smoked off to the suburb; a third flowering plant stood on the spot where the first had been taken. The second guinea was paid and the second chosen fuchsia adorned the drawing room of her second ladyship. The scene was repeated as new-comers saw and were attracted to the beauty of the plant. New chariots flew to the gates of old Lee's nursery grounds. Two fuchsias, young, graceful and bursting into healthy flower were constantly seen on the same spot in his repository. He neglected not to gladden the faithful sailor's wife by the promised gift, but ere the flower season closed three hundred golden guineas clinked in his purse, the produce of a single shrub of the widow in Wapping, the reward of the taste, decision, skill and perseverance of old Mr. Lee.

The authority for the story is given as 'Mr. Shepherd the respectable and informed conservator of the Botanical Gardens at Liverpool'.[15] It seems odd to say the least that this story should persist, that it changes from version to version is perhaps only to be expected and the versions that state the 'widow from Wapping' are probably due to the fact that the original story misspelt window. That Lee should have to resort to a story such as this to cover the fact that he really obtained the plant from Kew unofficially does not hold much cre- dence, as he was on very good terms with Aiton of Kew. One would think that if Lee had made up this story for some reason, he would have at least made sure the story could not be faulted and the sailor's wife would have said that her husband had brought it home from Brazil and not the West Indies as the story states.

The year 1789 saw a third species, *F. magellanica,* in cultivation and from this date until 1844 no less than eight more introductions were recorded and included: *F. lycoides* 1796, *F. arborescens* 1824, *F. microphylla* 1827, *F. fulgens* 1830, *F. corymbiflora* 1840, and *F. apetala, F. decussata* and *F. serratifolia* 1843-4.

As a nation it can be said with some pride that the British have been pre-eminent as plantsmen and hybridisers since the latter part of the sixteenth century and the possibilities of combining desirable features of the species, one with the other, were soon recognised. The earliest recording is said to be in 1832 when Bunney of Stratford, using almost certainly *F. magellanica or F. coccinea* as one parent of the cross, raised the first hybrid. Early records suggest that these two species were used extensively with other of the species, to produce, if nothing spectacular then at least something different. The real breakthrough occured in 1840 when the introduction of Venus Victrix was made by Cripps of Tunbridge Wells. This was thought to be a mutant seedling derived from *F. magellanica,* having a white tube, white sepals tipped with green and an almost blue corolla.

It has been said by some historians that almost all of the white tubed cultivars can claim descent from Venus Victrix and, though many would like to believe this sentimental association it is certain that similar mutations have occurred elsewhere and been used in selective crosses to achieve the modern white as we know it.

The latter half of the nineteenth century and the beginning of this century saw a rapid increase of raisers here and abroad. Principal raisers in Britain were Lye, Salter, Epps, Harrison, Standish, Story, Youell, Lane, Rundle, Veitch, Henderson, Bright and Banks. Outstanding and prolific raisers from the Continent were Lemoine, Rozain-Boucharlat, Cornelissen, Rehnelt, Henkel and Bonstedt. The raising of the first triphylla hybrids are not at all clearly documented in history but certainly Rhenelt, Henkel, Bonstedt and Lemoine were among the early raisers sending out the most attractive hybrids.

In Britain, from the nursery of Story, came the first white corollas, both single and double. These were later followed by the first striped corolla, adding fascinating possibilities for the future development of shape, form and colour. Hybridisers set to with a will and new introductions streamed onto a ready market.

Perhaps more than anyone, it was the head gardeners of Britain's great estates who most readily recognised the potential of the fuchsia as an exhibition plant. Pre-eminent among these was one James Lye, head gardener at Clyffe Hall, Market Lavington, Wiltshire, who apart from his mastery of fuchsia culture, raised a strain of fuchsia cultivars that were for ever to commemorate his name. The greater number of Lye's introductions possessed a distinctive waxy white tube and sepals of good substance and form, a characteristic that dominated and persisted in all his raisings and being so easily recognised they were soon said to have 'Lyes Hallmark'.

Most of his best introductions are with us still and without exception all are strong vigorous growers, and many make excellent show plants. This last quality was well illustrated by Lye himself when being photographed beside his huge specimen conicals and pyramids in the grounds of the estate upon which he worked. These cultural masterpieces were container grown and placed along the driveway leading to the house, a touch of exhibitionism which no doubt impressed visitors and guests. The overall measurements often exceeded 10 ft in height and 4 ft through the base from which they tapered symetrically to the top, Lye's talent as a grower and hybrid-iser was later emulated by his son-in-law George Bright, who despite the intervening war of 1914-18 managed to preserve a good selection of cultivars and indeed was introducing new cultivars as early as 1919.

During this period the fuchsia seemed to lose its former popu-larity and the decline of interest continued in Britain for some years, although a few enthusiasts later met and formed the Fuchsia Society in 1938. The first real revival of interest came from the United States of America, with the formation of the American Fuchsia Society in 1929. With typical American drive members set about the task of visiting Europe to collect specimen varieties and cultivars to be shipped back to initiate a breeding programme never before witnessed.

The Second World War was another great blow to the newly formed societies but both managed to retain the interest of their members by publishing literature whenever possible, and when hostilities ceased, the Americans once again returned to even greater efforts in hybridising techniques.

Each year more and more exciting new cultivars were reaching Britain and a great resurgence of interest swept through the country. The Fuchsia Society, by now renamed The British Fuchsia Society, although relatively low in members, had an enthusiastic team of officers and it is by these gentlemen that many old and forgotten varieties were hunted out and reintroduced.

British fuchsia enthusiasts will always be thankful to one of the Society's best-known hybridisers, Mr W.P. Wood, a man who quietly ignored the large American cultivars and set about breeding and raising a new race of cultivars capable of withstanding the rigours of an English winter. It is largely due to his work that permanent beds of fuchsias can be maintained in most gardens. Unfortunately

Mr Wood died suddenly in 1961 soon after the publication of his book *A Fuchsia Survey* in which he told of his hopes and aims for further improvement in hardy cultivars. During the course of his experiments he found that many cultivars thought to be tender were in fact comparatively hardy and could be used successfully as parents to increase size and generate a greater colour range in future hardy progeny.

The influx of American-bred cultivars has to some extent slowed down with the emergence of several British hybridisers such as Travis, Thornley and the late Cliff Gadsby, all of whom have achieved great success in raising cultivars more suitable to the unique British climate. Other British hybridisers who have produced some outstanding cultivars that have perhaps been for too long undisclosed to the wider public interest are Colville, Ryle, Dawson, Holmes, and more recently, Handley, Clyne and the late Wilf Tolley.

In England, the fuchsia owes much of its immense popularity to the British Fuchsia Society and, in particular to its founder members who, despite the restrictions of the Second World War, managed to keep alive the interest and declared objects of the young Society by publishing and distributing a yearbook to its widely scattered members during the years 1939-45. Much of this work was achieved by the then secretary Mr W.W. Whiteman, but unfortunately his untimely death in 1945 denied him the rewarding results of his dedicated service. His name and memory has since been perpetuated for all time by the Whiteman Memorial Medal of Honour, the Society's highest award for outstanding service to the Society and the fuchsia.

Undeterred by the consequences of past events the Society quickly reorganised and managed to put on a creditable show at the Royal Horticultural Hall, Westminster, once again demonstrating the pioneering determination to bring the fuchsia into its rightful position on the horticultural scene.

When one reflects upon today's membership, rapidly approaching 6,000, not even the most optimistic founder member could have anticipated the staggering success of their efforts. The annual London Show of the British Fuchsia Society has for many years now occupied an entire Royal Horticultural Society exhibition hall and shows are also held in Birmingham, Manchester and Reading.

In response to requests from members and officials concerned with competitive shows, the Society has revised and modernised its handbook of Judging Standards and has also recently instituted a judging examination, to guarantee that all plants will be appraised to a common set of standards. The end result has been a great asset to the Society and an enormous help to the exhibitor and judge alike.

The Society's activities over the years have done much to help and encourage local fuchsia groups all over the country and it has, with some justifiable pride, recently announced affiliations numbering 150. Of these 52 are specialist fuchsia societies which offer help and advice on any aspect of fuchsia culture and information on local growing conditions, etc. The more northern societies have contributed greatly with information on the hardiness of fuchsias with reports on trials undertaken to this end. This together with Royal Horticultural Society and British Fuchsia Society joint trials at Wisley Gardens have produced an impressive list of recommended garden cultivars.

Encouragement is also given to the increasing number of new hybridisers to submit their raisings to the BFS Floral Committee for assessment and award. For the novice raiser, this is an excellent opportunity to break into the realms of fame and recognition. Financial reward is not usually very great in this country, but a reasonable price can be negotiated between the raiser and a professional distributor.

British Fuchsia Society membership privileges include the Fuchsia Annual and periodic Bulletins containing topical news and views on all aspects of fuchsia culture, reports and events from local fuchsia groups, and also articles from the pens of successful growers. All members can take part in the yearly plant distribution scheme, this latter service being unique among floral societies in the world.

## Fuchsias in Other Countries

It is perhaps inevitable that the great resurgence of interest and popularity that is enjoyed by the fuchsia today, should have been initiated in America, albeit not that part of America from which most of the fuchsia species originate, but California, along the Pacific coast.

Here it was, in October 1929, that Miss Alice Eastwood, Curator of the California Academy of Science, Golden Gate Park, San Francisco, gathered together a number of fuchsia enthusiasts with the intention of forming a fuchsia society. That this was achieved will be underlined when shortly the American Fuchsia Society celebrates its fiftieth anniversary.

The early work of the young society was concerned with the compilation of a record of all the known fuchsias throughout the world, a mammoth task, which in 1934 resulted in the publication of Dr E.O. Essig's *Check List of Fuchsias*. This work carried nearly 2,000 entries covering nearly all of the known species and hybrids in cultivation at that time, as well as much information on the parentage of crosses made by the earlier hybridisers. This record has since been enlarged and kept up to date and the work of the

American Fuchsia Society in this respect was, some years ago, recognised by the International Society for Horticultural Science, when appointing them as the official International Registration Authority for Fuchsias, with responsibility for worldwide registration and nomenclature for fuchsias. Any hybridiser who wishes to register a new hybrid should write for information to the Chairman, Registration Committee, American Fuchsia Society, Hall of Flowers, Garden Center of San Francisco, Golden Gate Park, Ninth Avenue and Lincoln Way, San Francisco, California 94122.

Growers throughout the world will forever be indebted to the hybridisers in American, who from the mid 1930s produced an amazing amount of cultivars that did much to recapture a waning European interest.

The majority of these hybridisers produced quite prolific quantities of first-class cultivars and in doing so became household names among fuchsia enthusiasts, particularly in England. Among the very early hybridisers appear the names, Hazard & Hazard (Chang; Otherfellow), Evans & Reeves (Raindrops; Claire Evans; Mrs Lovell Swisher), Reiter (Falling Stars; Flying Cloud), Dr J.B. Lagen (Claret Cup; Halloween; Cascade), Schmidt (Carioca), Garson (Winston Churchill; RAF), Hodges (Powder Puff; Citation; Miss California), Niederholzer (Lucky Strike), Haag (Jack Acland; Duke of Wellington), Walker & Jones (Purple Heart; Peppermint Stick; Southgate; Pink Quartet; Tennessee Waltz; Party Frock), Tiret (Enchanted; Swingtime; Bridesmaid; Lace Pettitcoats. Sweet Leilani; Mamma Bluess; Angela Leslie; Leanora), Brand (Ruthie), Reedstrom (Marin Glow), Nelson (Rufus), Munkner (Curtain Call; Torch), Schnabel (Stella Marina; Sleigh Bells; Kings Ransome), Waltz (The Aristocrat; Blue Waves; So Big; Fort Bragg; Red Jacket; Shady Lane; Royal Velvet), Martin (Blue Pearl; Lady Beth; Red Ribbons; Sophisticated Lady; Normandy Bell; Orange Drops).

These then are the hybridisers and some of their cultivars that will hold nostalgic memories for many of our older enthusiasts when recalling the first time they grew some of those listed above, many of which are still seen each year at shows or in private collections, proof of their enduring quality. There have been many more names added to what is now a very long list of American hybridisers, all of whom have raised some very good cultivars indeed, and one hopes will continue to do so.

In 1941, around the area of Long Beach, California, a new fuchsia society was formed. This was named the California Fuchsia Society, and issued a monthly publication, *The Fuchsia Fan*, containing information on culture, pest control and reports on the activities of their branches which reach as far north as Santa Maria. In *The Fuchsia Fan* there had appeared a series of articles over a period of time by James Fairclo. Such was the popularity of these that the Society decided in 1946 to publish its first book which was entitled *A to Z on Fuchsias*, the same title as that used by James Fairclo for his articles. In addition, contributions by Victor Reiter, Jr, and Gus Niederholzer, with several others produced a very authoritative and popular book. This has since been revised and enlarged, and is still some 30 years later very much in demand.

In 1943 there came into being the National Fuchsia Society, establishing branches as far south as San Diego and having similar objects and activities as the California Fuchsia Society. It was in 1954 that these two Societies joined forces and became known as The California National Fuchsia Society, although in 1972 the Society was renamed The National Fuchsia Society.

So popular are fuchsias in California that one might be forgiven for mistaking a list of American cultivars for a gazetteer of place-names along the Pacific coast. There is hardly a place it would seem, from Fort Bragg to San Diego that has not had a fuchsia named after it, and many places inland from San Francisco and Los Angeles will be readily recognised as the names of fuchsia cultivars.

Many English growers profess to be rather envious of the Californian climate when they read that around the 'Bay' area of San Francisco most fuchsias experience no dormancy period and grow quite happily outside the whole year round. This part of California has a very mild and constant climate, the winter and summer temperatures fluctuating between 50-60°F with a relative humidity of about 85 per cent. This climate enables fuchsias to remain in bloom all year through and they are only retarded in their growth by pruning which is usually done during December and January.

Other parts of California are not quite so fortunate with such an ideal climate and temperatures of 115°F are usual in the Sacramento Valley, where the humidity is as low as 10 per cent and has to be augmented with mist spraying during the day to increase the humidity around the plants. Further south towards the coast again, in the Los Angeles basin, the humidity increases near the coastal region, but it is said to have five different climatic regions with temperatures of every degree.

Perhaps the most useful adjunct to the fuchsia grower in America is the shade house or lath house, and this would seem to be as necessary as the greenhouse is to the English grower. The shade house apart from creating a filtered sunlight also gives protection from hot, drying winds.

There has always been a free exchange of ideas, literature and cultivars between America and England and on occasion it has been our privilege to meet some of our American counterparts on their visits to England. These include Lilian Lee, who perhaps unknowingly did much to initiate this book, Ida Drapkin, who one suspects will be remembered by many of the BFS members on the occasion of her visit to the 1977 BFS show at Reading, Cathie and Mark Macdougal, who we remember hunting for Cathie's namesake at a BFS show at Horticultural Hall, Westminster, and lastly Al Stetler for his lecture and slide show at 'Thames Valley' and the plants of Cardinal.

Fuchsias in Holland

The Dutch Fuchsia Society or the *Nederlandse Kring van Fuchsia Vrienden* (Circle of Friends of the Fuchsia) was founded on 1 January 1965 with a membership totalling 38 and within three months had become affiliated to the Netherlands Royal Society of Horticulture and Botany. On 1 May of that year the first AGM was held in Utrecht and Mevrouw Meursing-Ferguson was elected as the first President of the Society. During their first year they exhibited displays of fuchsias at shows in Zwolle, The Hague and in Utrecht and in August of the following year they held their first society show in the Orangery of the Botanical Gardens at the University of Leiden. This show caused much interest, being viewed by some 7,000 people, 200 of whom had joined the society before the show closed. The Dutch Society is now well established and each year a party of their members have made a pilgrimage to the BFS show at Westminster as well as visiting several nurseries to collect new cultivars. In 1968 a seedling exhibited by Mr G. Hopgood which obtained a BFS Award of Merit at the London Show was named in honour of Mrs Meursing.

Fuchsias in New Zealand

There is an interesting story of an American gentleman who during service with the US Navy in 1943 found himself in Christchurch, New Zealand, and spent some time trying to find a fuchsia enthusiast who would be willing to accept a parcel of fuchsia plants after the war, sent at his expense, with the proviso that they would be put into commerce. When he was discharged from the Navy in 1945 Mr A.M. Larwick of Sacramento, California, did send several parcels of American fuchsias via Mr Victor Reiter, and these were eventually distributed throughout New Zealand and became so popular that a group of people in Auckland formed the New Zealand Fuchsia Society Inc. and the American sailor was elected a Fellow of the Royal New Zealand Institute of Horticulture for his efforts in introducing American fuchsias to New Zealand.

The New Zealand Society is not large, the bulk of the membership being from the Auckland area of North Island, although there are also some from South Island, their main contact with the society being a newsletter. Fuchsias are still gaining in popularity and the competitive show which is held around November time is also increasing in size.

Stewart Island, which is some 1,000 miles to the south, is not quite so fortunate in terms of climate and suffers a much harder winter than the north. The latter enjoys a long growing season which enables plants in outside situations to reach heights of 10 ft or more. Growers in this part of the country have to make use of shade houses for protection from sun and drying winds.

The Fuchsia Society of Rhodesia was formed in the early part of 1971 and, like the Dutch Society, in its early days confined its exhibiting techniques to arranging displays of fuchsias at various horticultural and agricultural shows, mainly in Salisbury, although they now hold their own competitive society show.

Fuchsias in Rhodesia

Summer temperatures often exceed 90°F with very little rain during May to October, so that this is a most trying time for fuchsia culture. The months of November through to April are the rainy months of the year and help greatly towards a flowering season of about nine months. Ground frosts are experienced around the end of July and can be quite severe with as much as 10-12 degrees of frost. Protection is given by mulching around the main stems of plants in outside plantings, although plants in tubs seem to survive without any extra protection.

It appears that one of the most popular ways of growing their plants is in hanging baskets, and one reads that these are made up of single plants as the climate and rate of growth is such that it prohibits the use of more than one plant per basket.

A few years ago a Fuchsia Society was formed in Adelaide, and will perhaps be the first of many. High temperatures, as one would expect, are the usual problems to overcome and in the Adelaide area summer temperatures can reach 100°F with very little humidity and the shade house has to be used during this time. These, Australian style, are wire netting structures which are covered with brushwood or palm fronds. In Western Australia in the area of Albany the average summer temperature is in the region of 75-80°F while further south in Tasmania a much more favourable climate enables plants to be grown far more successfully in the open.

Fuchsias in Australia

There are many other countries where fuchsias are grown quite successfully. These include Norway, Switzerland, Japan, Spain, Rumania and even (within the United States) Alaska, although none of these countries, as far as is known, have societies to help promote interest.

Other countries also have fuchsia societies. Canada has the British Columbia Fuchsia Society, and a few years ago one was formed in South Africa. Quite recently formed are the *Dansk Fuchsia Klub* in Denmark, the French Fuchsia Club, and also one in Germany. It is quite pleasing to know that there is a revival of interest in France and Germany, two countries that were very much concerned with our early hybrids.

## Notes

1. W.P. Wood, *A Fuchsia Survey*, Willims & Norgate, 1950.

2. Ibid.

3. W. Aiton, *Hortensus Kewensis,* 3 vols, 1789-99.

4. *Curtis's Botanical Magazine,* 1792.

5. *Floricultural Cabinet,* 1855.

6. James Lee, *An Introduction to the Science of Botany,* 4th edn, 1810.

7. James Britten and George Boulger, *A biographical index of deceased British and Irish botanists,* 2nd edn, Taylor and Francis, 1931.

8. G.E. Bate, *And So To Make a City Here,* Hounslow, Thomasons, 1948.

9. John Bowack, *The Antiquities of Middlesex,* 1705.

10. Hector Charles Cameron, *Sir Joseph Banks: the Autocrat of the Philosophers,* Batchworth Press, 1952.

11. *Botanist's Repository,* Plate 82.

12. Hector Charles Cameron, *Sir Joseph Banks.*

13. Thomas Jefferson, *Garden Book 1766-1842.*

14. W. Aiton, *Hortus Kewensis,* 2nd edn.

15. E.J. Wilson, *James Lee and the Vinyard Nursery, Hammersmith.*

# CHAPTER 2

# Propagation and Potting

The increase in one's collection, or stock, of plants can be accomplished in two ways, by seed and by cuttings. The first means, seed, is not used as a method of increasing stock of an existing cultivar because fuchsias do not come true from seed. Vegetative propagation by means of cuttings is therefore the only method that can be used to increase an existing plant stock, and keep it true to name.

Propagation from seed is invariably used only as a method of obtaining new, and one hopes, better cultivars and is fully detailed later in Chapter 9.

Vegetative propagation is best carried out by taking cuttings from stock fuchsia plants that are producing new growths following the annual period of dormancy. When this is done, the young spring growths root and develop in accordance with the natural sequence of growth patterns to a full adult life, in an uninterrupted progression throughout one complete growing season.

The plants that are used for producing cutting material (i.e. stock plants) should, if possible, be renewed each year as this does help to maintain a vigorous and healthy base from which to work. Old plants become hard and less inclined to produce new growths in any quantity. When renewing stock plants it is also adviseable to discard those that may have shown signs of deterioration in any form during the previous growing season.

The early season, or spring cutting is an ideal cutting for the amateur grower, although it must be said that many growers, including those in the trade, strike their cuttings in the autumn months when a plentiful supply of cutting material is available and rooting is possible without the aid of artificial heat. The autumn cutting, however, is quickly subjected to the winter dormancy period, in which growth all but ceases and a general hardening of wood takes place. This prematurely aged rooted cutting is at a disadvantage in the new season of growth as it is the nature of plant development to devote its energies to new top growth, usually to the detriment of the hard lower wood.

For the professional grower this type of propagation is necessary and practical if large quantities of plants are to be produced for the following season, but the cost of maintaining temperatures to provide conditions of uninterrupted growth throughout the winter months is not likely to commend itself to the average amateur. It is sometimes argued that autumn struck cuttings will make a larger plant, but this does not mean necessarily a better plant and this is frequently evident on the show bench each year.

Early season cuttings are best taken from rested stock plants. There is an annual rhythm for most plants and this should be allowed for by taking all pots of the current years growth outside when flowering has ended so that this natural dormancy can take place in normal winter conditions.

Light air frost is not likely to be dangerous but freezing conditions are, so precautions should be taken against these. Pots should be laid on their sides, to prevent rain constantly soaking the soil, and this will also help to induce the rest period rather more quickly.

Depending on the severity of winter conditions, the time to return the plants to the greenhouse will vary considerably; in the south they may well be left outside until the end of the year at which time they should be pruned back to three or four nodes on each branch. All weak growths should be cut right out and the soil surface should be thoroughly cleaned. If there are signs of worms having entered the pot, they should be searched out and removed. It is advisable to water the plants thoroughly with tepid water and allow this to drain off, after which they should be given an application of a general liquid fertiliser. The prepared plants must then be positioned over a source of gentle warmth on the greenhouse bench. If you have a cable-heated propagation bench so much the better; it is economical and very efficient.

The response to warmth after the cold treatment is most spectacular. Within a few weeks many vigorous new growths will develop and — contrary to the usual belief in waiting until two or three pairs of leaves have developed — the growths can be taken as soon as one pair of leaves and a growing tip is produced. The removal should be made with a razor blade close to the point of origin from the stock plant and the growth inserted directly into the rooting medium.

With this type of cutting it will be found that the stem is extremely short. For this reason it is inevitable that the two lower leaves will rest on the soil, but this is not detrimental in any way. The use of hormone rooting powder is academic, as the movement of plant hormones, particularly in young stems, provides all that is required for rooting to take place.

The merit of quickly rooting such small cuttings makes the early encouragement of laterals possible before stem extension becomes too great. Without a sturdy root system this early encouragement is not possible without causing a severe check to both root and shoot development.

The removal of a terminal bud activates two, and sometimes three, lateral buds below it. This creates a demand for more root to support the extra developing growths. Most of the plant's energy will be devoted to root production, and shoot growth will obviously be retarded until such time as a balance is achieved in the supply of organic material to the roots and, in turn, mineral and water to the shoots. Composts best suited to encourage good root action are described later.

Many growers strike their cuttings around the edge of a pot and, for the grower with only a few to strike this is an excellent way. Seed boxes, however, can accommodate 30-35 of the cuttings described above and are less likely to dry out as quickly as would those in pots.

Soil should be firmed down and made reasonably level before inserting the cuttings, and care should be taken to see that any depressions in the soil are not too deep as close contact between soil and the base of the cutting must be obtained. When the cuttings are all firmly in place the whole box of cuttings must be given a thorough watering, which is best done using a fine rose spray. No other waterings should be necessary until they are rooted. If however there should be signs of them drying out, a light overhead spray can be beneficial.

A soil temperature of 65-70°F will ensure fast rooting and cuttings can be ready for their first potting in 14 days. A moist atmosphere can be created by placing the tray of cuttings in a larger box and covering the whole with a sheet of glass. It is important to turn the glass over constantly to prevent water droplets that collect on the underside from dripping on to the cuttings. Each morning and evening should be sufficiently frequent for this.

The grower who possesses a soil-warmed propagating bench will be able to cope with a much larger quantity of cuttings at one time. It is usual with this method of striking cuttings to insert them directly into the bed of prepared rooting medium over the soil-warming cable which, for the obvious reason of economy, should be thermostatically controlled. The nurseryman, or even the keen amateur, can combine a mist propagating unit with the soil-warmed bench with which it is possible to root fuchsia cuttings in seven days. However, few amateurs will find this ingenious system necessary for

27

small batches of cuttings. The soil-warmed bench is nevertheless a useful addition to the greenhouse and can be very economical if one or two points are observed. A covering of plastic sheeting can be used to conserve both warmth and moisture, so conducive to fast rooting. This should be constructed on a frame which is easily dismantled when not required. Another tip is to put each cutting in its own small plastic pot of rooting compost and these in turn are placed in a plastic seed tray. These should then be placed on the propagating bench, each tray side touching the one next to it. If the whole bench is filled with trays it will be found that a considerable amount of heat will be retained beneath the trays and moisture loss from the bench will also be very much reduced. Used in this way a heated propagating bench will prove invaluable to even the smallest greenhouse.

When young cuttings are rooted they will take on a lively, fresher look. This is a signal to admit more air, even during the rooting period. This should be done for short periods to let out excess moisture, but when fully rooted, air can be given all day and closed down at night. After a day or two, if the young plants respond to more air, the cover can be left off and preparations for potting can begin.

To those with little or no special facilities for raising early cuttings but who might nevertheless wish to produce the odd plant or two from an existing fuchsia, this can be done, preferably in mid season, by detaching stems from parent plant with a heel (see figure 2.1). These are then inserted in pots of moist, sandy soil to root. If this method is used, some care must be exercised as it can damage the parent plant.

Semi- and hardwood cuttings (see Figure 2.2) will root equally well by making a clean cut just below a leaf node. Lower leaves should be removed from about a quarter of the length of the cuttings and then inserted around the edge of a deep flower pot filled with a sandy compost. These can be put into the frame and shaded from direct sunshine, where an occasional spray with clear water is beneficial. Conditions for encouraging quicker rooting may be created by fixing a plastic bag over the pot and cuttings, which are then rooted indoors.

So-called suckers are often available and provide an easy means of increase. Such growths originate underground and can be removed complete with roots, potted up, or even planted direct into a garden location.

The rooting of several semi-hardwood cuttings in strips of polythene sheeting is an ingenious method of increasing stock without a lot of trouble or special conditions. Cuttings are taken and prepared in the usual manner of semi-hardwoods:

Figure 2.1
Stem Detached
from Parent
Plant and
Showing a Heel

Prepare a strip of polythene measuring 6 in by 8 in and lay damp sphagnum moss along the top half of its length. Into this lay the prepared cuttings 1in apart, keeping the top leaves clear of the edge. Fold up the lower half of the polythene over the moss and cuttings until both edges meet, then, starting at one end, roll the strip up firmly to the other end and secure with a tie or elastic bands at top and bottom. Placed near a window, rooting is fairly fast. Pot up as soon as this is observed.

An interesting way of increasing the supply of young plants from a limited amount of cutting material is the internodal cutting (see Figure 2.3B). A stem carrying several pair of leaves can be induced to provide a rooted growth from every leaf axil. The growing tip can be taken as an ordinary nodal cutting (see Figure 2.3A). The remainder of the stem is then cut into several pieces, severed about ½ to 1in below each pair of leaves, and each piece is prepared as

Figure 2.2
A Full-length
Semi-hardwood
Cutting

follows. The stem immediately above each pair of leaves is fore-shortened to just above the leaf axils (see Figure 2.4). The task is then to split the remaining short stem longitudinally down between the leaves, thus giving two pieces of split stem, each having a leaf attached (see Figure 2.3C). Prepare all the material in a like manner and insert each piece into the rooting medium up to the nodal swelling, but leaving the tip and leaf axil just clear of the surface. Rooting takes place from the lower uncut side of the stem. Given optimum conditions, some dozen or more growing plants from a single stem can be rooted sufficiently well to be potted up within four weeks. Cuttings taken from the lower end of the stem or branch will be of harder wood and will take a little longer to root (see Figure 2.3D).

Striking cuttings without the aid of heat or the facilities of a greenhouse must be delayed considerably. In mid April or even later, growth from the current season should be taken about 1 in long and inserted into a prepared compost. Again seed boxes are the ideal containers, and these should be placed within a larger box covered

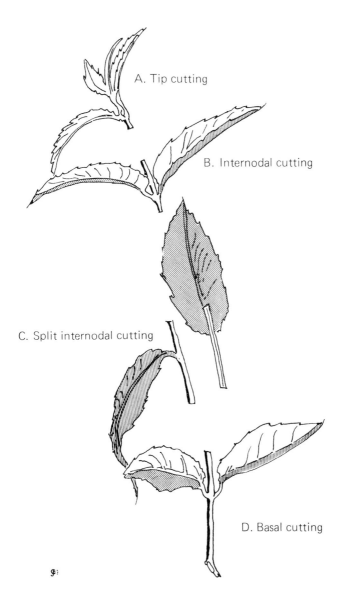

Figure 2.3
Stem Cut Into
Sections Showing
Four Possible
Types of
Cuttings

A. Tip cutting

B. Internodal cutting

C. Split internodal cutting

D. Basal cutting

with a sheet of glass, the whole then being transferred to a cold frame. Some shading might be necessary on bright sunny days and the glass should be turned every day. Watering should not normally be necessary until the cuttings have rooted, but a constant watch is advisable, particularly after several sunny days. Rooting cuttings under these conditions will take more or less three weeks, after which they must be potted up into pots of not more than 3 in diameter, thoroughly watered, and returned to the cold frame. The frame should be kept closed for a day or two, then given more air. Watering must be watched more closely, and the use of overhead spraying is beneficial on bright sunny days, though attention should also be paid to a light shading on the glass to help prevent scorching

Figure 2.4
Cuttings Trimmed
ready for insertion
into Rooting Medium

of the young leaves. Early spring can be a trying time for young soft growth, with frequent showers followed by bursts of sunshine, which if ignored can quickly ruin a batch of young plants.

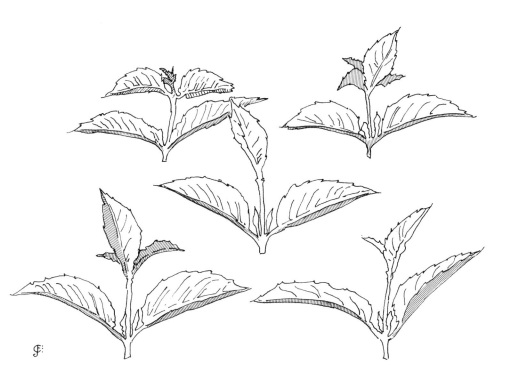

Another rather novel way to strike just a few cuttings for anyone who does not have the facilities of a greenhouse, is the sweet-jar method. The very large type of plastic sweet-jar can, when washed and dried, be used as a mini greenhouse. A small plastic pot, of a size that will pass through the neck of the jar, should be filled with rooting compost and well watered. When this has drained off, four or five cuttings (see Figure 2.5) may then be inserted and the whole is then placed on the upturned lid of the jar. The jar itself is then placed over the pot and cuttings, and screwed down onto the lid. The cuttings should need no further attention until they are rooted, which takes three to four weeks. Any airtight jar of similar size may be used.

Figure 2.5
Group of General Purpose Cuttings, Sometimes Referred to as Ultra-greentips

Many failures in pot culture can be attributed to careless practices, none more so than the use of dirty pots. The old soil can contain

Potting

harmful bacteria and the clean removal of a soil ball can be prevented by roots clinging to the ingrained dirt. Scouring out old pots is tiresome but the effort must be made if the health and well being of your plants is to be maintained. Plastic pots are less difficult to keep clean but they too must be well washed and rinsed out. It is usual to employ plastic pots when using soil less compost and clay pots for loam-based composts, but the reverse order is sometimes used, and apparently with success. Watering, however, needs to be carefully watched.

While the crocking of plastic pots is not quite so necessary, clay pots, by reason of their large drainage holes, do need this service. This means placing a piece of broken pot archside up over the drainage hole so that water can drain easily away yet retain the soil. Several pieces should be used in the case of larger pots to improve drainage.

When potting rooted cuttings it must be stressed that to over-pot is detrimental to good root development, so a 2 in or at most a 2½ in pot is used. Fill it about half way up with fresh, moist compost and then gently lift out the young plant from the rooting medium, carefully levering under the roots to avoid any breakage of the delicate root system. Spread the roots evenly over the compost in the pot, and gauging the correct depth, add more compost to cover them. The stem should be buried only as deep as it was in the rooting material.

The secret of all good potting is to pot evenly all the way up, leaving no cavities or voids between the soil ball and the sides of the pot. Firm the compost by finger only, and finish off with a level surface, leaving sufficient space for watering purposes.

The first watering for newly potted cuttings is best carried out by the capillary method, in much the same way as one does with seedlings in a seed tray, by partial immersion, allowing the water to rise gradually to the surface from below rather than from an overhead watering. Later, when the roots have taken hold, normal watering can be employed.

For a few days after potting, the young plants will need a moist, warm atmosphere to help them readjust, after which they must take their place in the airier conditions on the greenhouse staging. When the plant is growing steadily a visual check on root development is necessary. Turn the plant out of its pot and, if the roots are running freely to the sides, shift to a larger pot. Never allow developing roots to overcrowd small pots, as this leads to premature hardening of the stem, and is a serious check to its future wellbeing.

Preparatory to potting-on, ensure that you have ample compost and clean pots to hand. Turn out the plant with its ball of soil and place on fresh soil in the larger pot. Work more soil between the side of the pot and soil ball firmly and evenly. A thin stick or stiff plant label may be used to ensure that no cavities or voids are left, but very great care must be taken not to damage the roots. The finished soil level can be a little higher up the stem, but do not overdo it. Again, finger pressure only is used to firm and level. At no time should the compost be compacted. Use just enough pressure to ensure that the young plant stands upright in the pot, as subsequent watering will help to consolidate the compost. Always see that the plant to be moved on has been watered previously: this greatly assists clean removal.

Progressive potting must at all times be taken in gradual stages. Do not be tempted to overmeasure the next size of pot in an endeavour to save time. Small amounts of fresh soil added frequently will ensure that the roots will seek out efficiently the amount given, and produce a vigorous root system.

If all goes well, late spring will herald final potting: your plant is strong and healthy and the roots are vigorous. Much firmer potting is now acceptable. A 6 in pot is adequate to see the average first season plant through a full growing season to flower production. When a plant reaches the stage at which it is able to flower, a degree of root crowding in the pot is accepted as an encouragement to flowering. But there are limitations to this.

The situation arises occasionally when a plant has developed so well that re-potting is made difficult by sheer mass of low growth. This foliage impedes the action of working new soil down the sides of the pot and it becomes necessary to employ quite a different technique. This is only likely to be on the final potting, so take a 6 in pot, crock if necessary and add soil to the height on which would rest the ball of rooted soil. Now take an empty pot (the outside measurement being as close as possible to the size of the rootball), place in the exact centre and fill the gap between the two pots with fresh compost (this can be packed down quite firmly). Then remove the centre pot carefully and drop the plant in the space provided. Firmly press down and add a little loose soil to the surface for levelling up.

The practice of growing plants in pots leads eventually to exhaustion of soil minerals, but this situation will not normally arise until the final pot is full of roots, at which stage a regular programme of dilute liquid fertiliser is applied.

**Composts for Potting**

The standard John Innes potting composts, which were evolved at the John Innes Horticultural Institute in the 1930s, are possibly still the best composts available for container-grown plants if made strictly to formula. Unfortunately the most important ingredient, pastureland turves, are almost at a premium, and all too often one finds that almost any kind of so-called topsoil is being put to use as a substitute, at times with disastrous results for the unsuspecting recipient. It is for this reason that many soil less composts are now offered and used, having gained a popular hold on the market, many brand names being available to the present-day gardener.

Loam used for making a batch of compost to the John Innes recommendations should, if one keeps strictly to the formula, be sterilised, but if a reliable and convenient source of loam is available that is not sterilised it can be used for growing fuchsias and may well prove to be better than many ready-prepared products claiming to be made to the JI standards of quality.

*John Innes No. 1 Suitable for Cuttings* — To prepare two bushels take:

7 seed trays of sifted loam
3 seed trays of sifted moist peat (hort. grade)
2 seed trays of dry coarse sand
(a standard seed tray measures 14" x 8½" x 3")

To this must be added:

3 oz hoof and horn
3 oz superphosphate of lime        = JI base
1½ oz sulphate of potash
1½ oz ground chalk

Efficient mixing of the above materials is important and is best arrived at by first mixing the fertilisers to the sand. Spread the loam over a flat surface, cover with a layer of peat, then add the fertiliser/sand mix, spreading evenly over the sandwiched heap. The whole must then be turned over thoroughly several times.

John Innes base fertiliser can be purchased ready mixed if so desired, in which case 7½ oz of base fertiliser plus 1½ oz of ground chalk is equivalent to that detailed above. Note that hoof and horn can be replaced by nitroform, a modern fertiliser that is slowly released and continually available over a period of six months. 1 oz of nitroform is equal to the nitrogen content of 3 oz of hoof and horn. If purchasing a ready mixed JI base, it would be a wise precaution to check and use the maker's recommended weight measure per bushel.

*John Innes No. 2* — For potting rooted cuttings into and up to 3½ in pots. To the same quantities of loam/peat/sand as previously detailed add:

6   oz hoof and horn
6   oz superphosphate of lime
3   oz sulphate of potash
3   oz ground chalk

*John Innes No. 3* — For potting on into intermediate and final pots. To the same quantities of loam/peat/sand as previously detailed add:

9   oz hoof and horn
9   oz superphosphate of lime
4½ oz sulphate of potash
4½ oz ground chalk

Large specimen plants occupying large containers could well require JI No. 4 for any final potting. For this take the same quantities of loam, peat and sand and add:

12   oz hoof and horn
12   oz superphosphate of lime
6    oz sulphate of potash
6    oz ground chalk

Should there be a preference for a more modern type of growing medium a loamless compost can very easily be made that is suitable for fuchsias.

Sphagnum moss is the most usual type of peat used in the preparation of soil less growing media. It contains a little nitrogen, phosphate, potash and some of the trace elements, but these are so low in value as to be virtually of no consequence, and can be essentially considered a sterile medium. It can however, hold water up to 15 times its own weight, allows easy access for root penetration and development, and is clean, light and easy to handle.

Despite the water absorption qualities of peat, drying out is rather more rapid than with soil-based composts in hot, dry conditions and, in extreme conditions can be very difficult to re-wet. All too often water floods through the container, leaving root-compacted compost, still very dry in the middle. Some manufacturers of soil less composts include a quantity of ground clay to increase the buffering capacity of their products. A recent introduction to the English market is sintered fireclay, a product of high porosity which can absorb water quickly, and help to prevent water from running straight through over-dry composts by later releasing it gradually and evenly through the bulk. Suited ideally for inclusion in soil less composts, it is graded from 1-6 mm and can be used as a complete replacement for the usual grit aggregate, or be used half and half. It also has the quality of being chemically inert.

There are some problems of which the grower should be wary, not least the very acid state of peat. This is particularly so with sphagnum moss types, being recorded as low as 3.7 on the pH (potential hydrogen) scale. It is therefore necessary to add quite large amounts of lime to neutralise or correct to a pH level of around 6.5-7.

This at once poses the question of possible unfavourable reaction from certain fertiliser ingredients when in contact with lime. Selection is therefore important when using a prepared compound fertiliser: make sure it is suitable to add to soil less composts. On no account should organic fertilisers be used in soil less mixes, as these can lead to a build up of toxicities under certain conditions.

Any dry fertiliser proclaiming its suitability for soil less mixes may be used, and carbonate of lime is added by the purchaser when preparing the compost to ensure a correct pH level. This is detailed more fully under nutrients.

Also available are specialist compound fertiliser packs formulated specifically for peat composts. Each is sufficient to make two bushels of compost, and suitable quantities of lime are combined in the formula as a whole.

Plant foods are present in both quick and slow acting forms, together with the necessary trace elements, giving a balanced blend of all the essentials for healthy plant growth.

For anyone who wishes to mix their own soil less compost the following instructions for a two bushel mix has our personal recommendation.

If the peat is purchased in compressed bales it will be very dry and lumpy. This must be broken down, and is achieved by thorough saturation of the required quantity with water, after which it should be allowed to drain off and then rubbed through a sieve.

Using a two-gallon household bucket gives a fairly accurate measure for both peat and sand. Two bushels equal 16 gallons.

Spread 1½ bushels of moist sieved peat on a level surface, then cover with half a bushel of cornish or river grit, or better still use half grit and half sintered fireclay. This must now be mixed thoroughly. The addition of sufficient nutrients correctly balanced is all that is required to convert this material into an ideal growing medium. The following inorganic fertiliser mix is sufficient for two bushels.

10 oz dolomite lime
10 oz carbonate of lime
4 oz superphosphate
1½ oz nitroform
1 oz trace element frit 253A
½ oz potassium nitrate
½ oz potassium sulphate

The above items should be well mixed together then added to the main bulk and thoroughly mixed once again. The importance of the mixing process cannot be over-stressed as all ingredients must be evenly distributed for optimum results. Prepare the compost 24 hours before use for the best results, and use within a week or two of preparation.

**Compost for Rooting Cuttings**

It is often stated that a suitable medium for rooting cuttings can be made by mixing equal quantities of peat and sharp sand together, and it must be admitted that it is a very tempting proposition for the average amateur, but it is also one that should not be undertaken too lightly or without careful consideration of possible later ill effects. First, if one considers that a mature plant requires a growing medium with a pH of 6.5-7 to grow properly, it will take little thought to realise that a cutting trying to put out roots in a very acid medium is going to be far from happy. The addition of sharp sand to peat makes little difference to the pH value, which as previously outlined is often as low as 3.7- 4. Therefore it is recommended that rooting mediums should be corrected to a pH level of 6.5-7 for satisfactory results.

Another point that should be considered is the length of time that the rooted cutting will remain in the rooting medium before being removed and potted-up. The amateur grower, for many reasons, is not always able to effect a quick removal from the rooting medium and any prolonged delay in doing so could well result in severe nutritional deficiency if the medium is of sand and peat only. Such cuttings rarely make good show plants when subjected to this early treatment.

Fuchsia cuttings root quite happily and equally as fast in John Innes No. 1 compost, which has the advantage of containing sufficient plant nutrients to sustain a robust root system and sturdy vegetative growth, plus a greater margin of time before potting-on requirements become urgent.

Another satisfactory rooting medium is the self-mix loamless compost described earlier for potting. Excellent results can be expected and have proved to be a better proposition for the amateur with a limited amount of time.

### Loam-based Seed Compost (JI Standard)

Serious hybridisers, having carefully gathered their seed, will no doubt seek the best possible compost in which to raise them. Therefore it should be free of any agency likely to transmit disease, must allow easy access for root penetration, and be perfectly drained.

The John Innes formula for seed compost requires partial sterilisation of its loam content and for that reason alone is not usually practical as a home mix for the average amateur, unless of course it may be thought a good investment to purchase one of the several home sterilising units available at many of the larger garden sundriesmen. It is with this possibility in mind, that the following formula is given:

2 parts by bulk of sifted partially sterilised loam
1 part by bulk of sifted moist horticultural peat
1 part by bulk of sifted dry horticultural sand

To each bushel of the above mix is added:

1½ oz superphosphate of lime
3/8 oz carbonate of lime (ground chalk)

It is always advantageous to mix the fertilisers with the dry sand first, before adding to the loam and peat. The whole should then be thoroughly mixed until all items are evenly distributed.

### Seed Compost (Self Mix)

Seed can be raised successfully in a peat and sand mix, which has the immediate virtue of being not only simple to prepare but also free of harmful organisms. Large amounts are not normally required by the amateur, so that a bushel is a quantity likely to be sufficient.

The 2 gallon household bucket is probably the most convenient measure for both peat and sand and is therefore used here:

2 x 2 gallons moist granular horticultural peat
2 x 2 gallons dry horticultural sand

to which is added:

1   oz superphosphate of lime
5   oz dolomite lime
3   oz Osmocote fertiliser* (NPK 15-12-15)
½ oz trace element frit 253A

* Osmocote is sold under two types, one is long term, the other is short term. In the above mixture the short term is used.

Before attempting to mix the above, the peat must be rubbed through a 3/8 or 1/4 in sieve, to achieve the required texture suitable for seed. Mix the fertiliser to the sand before adding to the peat. Thoroughly mix the whole to ensure an even distribution of the ingredients.

**Potential Hydrogen Scale**

The range of pH values is given for convenience within a scale of 0-14. The figure 7 corresponds to neutrality, all values less than that being acid and all those above alkaline.

Degree of acidity is dependent on the concentration of hydrogen ions in a soil solution and can be determined with reasonable accuracy with a simple, commercially available, outfit.

Concentrations increase or decrease 10 times for each whole number of pH change, the scale being logarithmic. Therefore a pH of 5 is 10 times as acid as pH 6, and pH 4 is 100 times as acid as pH 6. Intermediate values are expressed as decimals.

One whole unit of change on the pH scale represents a massive shift in practical terms. A pH of 6.5 is acid but acceptable for most plant subjects, including the fuchsia. A further drop to pH 6 would reach the point of acidity at which only acid-loving subjects such as heathers, azaleas, etc., would thrive.

Although greater emphasis has been given to acid conditions, it must also be remembered that indiscriminate applications of lime can shift the scale to one of extreme alkalinity, producing again deficiencies in essential plant foods. Briefly, pH 6 is too acid and pH 8 is too alkaline for most decorative container-grown subjects.

# CHAPTER 3

# Fertilisers and Nutrients

A basic understanding of the nutrients required by plants is of importance if specimens are to be produced that are healthy, well formed, and with abundance of good leaf and flower.

Plants that are grown in pots and containers, particularly if grown under glass or some other type of protected area, are in many ways at a disadvantage when compared with those growing outside in the open ground. The root system is nearly always restricted and in consequence the supply of nutrients to the plant is totally dependent on a sustained supplementary feeding programme. From the final pot stage, it is essential that nutrients leached from the soil through constant watering are regularly replaced.

A common fallacy that exists among many growers concerns the plant requirements of nitrogen and potash. One often hears the advice 'feed with nitrogen in the early stages of growth, then switch to high potash when all stopping of side shoots is completed'. Unfortunately, although this advice is near to being correct, it is only a very small part of the story.

The importance of the pH level of the compost in which the plant is growing cannot be overstressed, for it is the basis of any good feeding programme. If the pH is wrong the plant could well be deprived of nutrients even though they are regularly fed to the plant. It was mentioned earlier that composts should be corrected to a pH of 6.5-7, since this is considered as the level at which most nutrients are at their maximum availability. Thus the first step of an efficient feeding programme is to make sure of a correct pH level.

The nutrients required by plants for healthy vigorous growth are usually divided into two groups. The 'macro' nutrients are those that are required in large quantities and the 'micro' nutrients, sometimes referred to as trace elements, are required in very much smaller quantities although being just as important to the wellbeing of the plant.

The macro nutrients, most of which are included as the base fertiliser when mixing the potting medium, include nitrogen, potassium, calcium, magnesium, phosphorus and sulphur. In addition the plant obtains oxygen, hydrogen and carbon from the photosynthesic transformation of water and carbon dioxide.

Micro nutrients or trace elements should also be included when making up the potting medium, particularly if the medium is of the soil less type where inert materials are used. These are usually included in the form of frits, which are preparations of the particular nutrients with finely ground glass, the formation of which allows the nutrients to be released slowly over a long period of time.

The recommended frit 235A is ideal for use with soil less composts and is composed of:

   2 per cent boron
   2 per cent copper
  12 per cent iron
   5 per cent manganese
0.13 per cent molybdenum
   4 per cent zinc
Made up to 100 per cent with sodium and silicon

Many beginners become bemused when faced with the problem of choosing a fertiliser or nutrient. They mostly know that plants growing in pots do require supplementary feeding but hesitate to give this because they do not know which one does what, or how much or how often to apply. Briefly, every item mentioned above is required to ensure that they receive an adequacy for their metabolism.

### Calcium

This is essential at the site of cell division for the growth of meristems and root tips. The absorption of nitrogen is also reliant on sufficient calcium being available. Many fuchsias that show a decrease in leaf size as the season progresses, often attributed to high levels of potash, may well be suffering from a calcium deficiency.

A valuable source of calcium is obtained from carbonate of lime. Another is Dolomite lime (magnesium carbonate) which also contains about 10 per cent magnesium. Both are invaluable for inclusion in soil less potting mediums based on peat to raise the pH level.

### Magnesium

This element is required by plants as an activator of enzymes. Phosphorous is one element that requires an adequate supply of magnesium in the medium, to enable it to be fully mobile within the

the plant. High levels of potassium can induce a magnesium deficiency, but this can be remedied, should it occur, by applications of magnesium sulphate (Epsom salts, 9.7 per cent Mg as $MgSO_4 \cdot 7H_2O$) either as a foliage spray (½ oz to 2 gals water) or by inclusion in the medium. Another source of magnesium is kieserite (16 per cent $MgSO_4 \cdot H_2O$) which is best applied by including it when making up the medium as it is not readily soluble.

### Phosphorus

Phosphorus is another element that is vital to plant metabolism, especially in the growth of roots in young plants. Superphosphate is the usual form included in potting mediums being about 9 per cent phosphorus by weight.

### Sulphur

This element is only required in small quantities by plants and is found in plant proteins. Potassium sulphate is the usual source of supply containing 17 per cent sulphur.

### Nitrogen

This is vital to the production of vegetative growth, i.e., leaf and stems. It must be adequately available throughout the growing season to maintain the quality of the plant, a fact that seems to be overlooked by many exhibitors in their anxiety to increase flower production in their show plants. It is a fallacy that when the supply of potash is increased, the supply of nitrogen should cease. If a plant requires any nutrient at all, then it will be needed all the time (see potassium).

In excess, nitrogen will increase the size of the plant cells, which ultimately raises the water content of the plant. This can make the plant more susceptible to attack by pests and, in an unprotected situation, to frost. Used judiciously, nitrogen will preserve a certain softness in the foliage that is very desirable, particularly if the plant is to be used for exhibition.

A useful form of nitrogen which is ideal for inclusion in soil less potting mediums is nitroform (38 per cent N) which is a slow-release synthetic fertiliser, providing nitrogen to the plant for up to six months after application.

Urea (46 per cent N) is another compound invaluable for use in liquid feeds and is very quick acting. A further very useful source of nitrogen is potassium nitrate which is particularly good as it combines two major elements (see Table 3.1).

### Potassium

The role of potassium in plants is one of extreme importance, which is probably why many growers are guilty of applying too much. It is essential to the synthesis of chlorophyll and to satisfactory rates of photosynthesis. It also acts as an osmotic regulator, being used to counteract high levels of nitrogen. If high levels of potassium are fed continually, an induced magnesium deficiency may occur, although this can be rectified by application of magnesium sulphate. Many growers who adopt the principle of giving massive doses of potash to their plants to encourage flower production, forget that in doing so they will probably inhibit the action of any remaining nitrogen in the media and that if nitrogen does cease to be available, there will be a drastic change in the appearance of the plant. It will become hard and woody, the leaves will be smaller, and the older leaves may be lost, the whole plant taking on a rather stunted appearance.

Potassium, together with phosphorus and nitrogen, should be fed to plants in equal proportions for the best results in the earlier stages of growth, when the plant is being built up and side growths are still required for shaping purposes. When this part of the plant's training is completed and further growth is allowed to proceed (usually about four more pairs of leaves) to eventual flowering, the feed can be altered to include extra potassium, but on no account should the quantities of the other two elements be reduced, or withdrawn completely, because although the plant does benefit at this time from an increase of potassium it does still require the other two elements for satisfactory growth. It is suggested that the ratio should be 1:1:2 and it is usually beneficial to give an application of magnesium sulphate about once a month to ensure adequate magnesium ions in the soil solution. Many experienced growers who practice high levels of liquid feeding find that it is very beneficial to the well-being of the plant to give regular applications of clear water between feeds to help control the build-up of undesirable residues in the media.

## Iron

This micro-nutrient is very necessary for chlorophyll production and photosynthesis and although required in only small quantities is nevertheless a most important nutrient. Iron deficiency symptoms can be induced by an excess of phosphorus, zinc and lime, and conversly, by a potassium deficiency, though few fuchsia growers are likely to be troubled by the latter. 'Chlorosis', as the deficiency is known, can be controlled by the use of iron sequenstrene, if all else fails. Chlorotic conditions can be recognised by the yellowing, usually interveinal, of the leaf due to lack of chlorophyll formation.

## Boron

Deficiency symptoms of this element can be many and varied,

though fortunately few are common to the fuchsia. It can be responsible for die-back. Boron is, however, essential for the uptake of calcium and therefore should, if for no other reason, be maintained at adequate levels.

### Molybdenum

In an acid medium this can become unavailable, a state that is symptomised by a mottled chlorosis. A correction of the pH level should ensure that this does not become a problem.

### Copper

A deficiency of this element can be the cause of the premature fall of leaves and flowers, though it is not usually the reason for this in fuchsias.

### Zinc

This is an element that is important to the regulation of sugars and the decomposition of carbon dioxide and water.

Table 3.1: Inorganic Fertilisers

|  | Nitrogen | Phosphate | Potash | Dilution |
|---|---|---|---|---|
| Urea | 46% | — | — | 1 oz to 6 gals |
| Ammonium sulphate | 20% | — | — | 1 oz to 2 gals |
| Ammonium nitrate | 35% | — | — | 1 oz to 5 gals |
| Potassium nitrate | 13% | — | 46% | 1 oz to 2 gals |
| Potassium sulphate | — | — | 48% | 1 oz to 1 gal |
| Mono ammonium phosphate | 11% | 48% | — | 2½ oz to 2 gals |

A cheap and useful compound fertiliser can be made by mixing together, in equal proportions by weight, potassium nitrate and urea. These are used at 1 oz to 6 gallons of water, and are forms in which the elements are quickly available to the plant, as results will show. It is non-caustic and can be used as a foliar feed.

The excellent John Innes liquid feed can also be made in bulk form by mixing the following ingredients by weight and using at a rate of 1 oz per gallon:

15 oz ammonium sulphate
2¾ oz potassium nitrate
2¼ oz mono ammonium phosphate

This is sufficient for 20 gallons of quick-acting complete fertiliser. But keep away from the foliage since ammonium sulphate is caustic.

The above inorganic fertilisers are highly concentrated and should not be used to excess. Too much of a particular element can be more injurious than a deficiency, as it cannot easily be rectified.

A plant growing within the restriction of a pot or container will eventually exhaust all the available nutrients contained in the growing media, so that a regular programme of supplementary feeding must be undertaken to sustain steady growth.

**Supplementary Feeding**

Many beginners will no doubt be fascinated by confidential claims that certain nutrient elements given in straight applications produce miraculous results in terms of either rapid growth or spectacular flower production. Such claims are ill advised, particularly for the novice, and should be ignored until such time as a greater personal growing experience can determine that a particular nutrient deficiency is obvious in a plant to warrant such drastic measures. Diagnosis of deficiency symptoms is, at best, no more than an intelligent guess in many cases, as several different deficiencies can exhibit the same symptoms.

This can give rise to possible errors of judgement, resulting in excess of one nutrient element causing a deficiency in another; a situation leading to utter confusion and disappointment. It is more prudent to rely on the expertise of specialist firms who produce compound fertilisers scientifically blended either in a dry form or as a concentrated liquid.

Liquid fertilisers, although much more expensive than dry, are more convenient to the amateur as their use combines watering and feeding in one operation, thus giving a better overall distribution of nutrients. There are two types available, those of solid chemicals for dissolving in water and those of liquids to be diluted in water.

The frequency of feeding pot plants is to a large extent dependent upon the frequency of watering. Under normal circumstances where water is given, say, two or three times a week, a recommended amount of feeding every week or ten days is satisfactory, but given conditions where the plant is subjected to rapid drying out and water is a twice daily need, fertilisers are washed out of the growing media and must be replenished more often. Given such conditions feeding every other day at half strength is acceptable. One or two applications of clear water is advisable, particularly when using a soil less media, to ensure that complete saturation of the root ball is effected prior to applying the fertiliser dose.

Different periods of growth and development of a plant will naturally demand more of one nutrient element than another and this is provided for by some makers of complete fertilisers, who alter the composition of the three major elements to satisfy the requirement for vegetative growth or promotion of ripe wood and eventual flowering. The period of change is usually implemented when all stopping or pinching is completed.

The production cost of highly active ingredients used in the manufacture of compound liquid fertilisers is reflected in the price we pay and, to a point, is indicative of overall quality and economy of use. Dilution rates are determined scientifically to give optimum growing results, and there is no merit in being over generous in measure.

# CHAPTER 4

# Choosing Plants

Selection of cultivars with a capability of displaying good qualities for exhibition purposes, requires an appreciation and prior knowledge of growth habit to assess its adaptability to a specific plant form definition.

The impractability in certain situations of cultivars with a tendency to lax pendulous growth, is perhaps too obvious but there are many other considerations that make one cultivar more practical than another for show work. The Bush and Shrub show classes are without doubt the most popular and competition is such that the right choice of plant is of paramount importance to the intending showman.

A visit to any of the major fuchsia shows staged throughout the country during the season is a way of adding to one's knowledge of correct selection of cultivar for a particular form. It will be noticed amongst the more successful entries that favoured characteristics include sturdy short jointed growth, an ability to branch freely, good foliage overall, and above all a profusion of fresh flower of equal distribution.

The popularity of shrub growth as against bush growth will immediately be apparent, due partly to the stricter control of development and culture required in the bush form. It is however appreciated that the novice grower will gain experience from the more easily managed shrub, which allows the retention and encouragement of additional growths springing from the root system to build the resultant size and shape.

The attraction of a particular flower size, colour or form, will naturally influence a choice, and as much as we all have an affection for the exotic flower of great dimensions, it will eventually become evident to the observer that plants producing these exceptional blooms are ineffectual as show specimens and are rarely if ever seen on the show bench. Disappointing as it may be, appeasement quickly follows on acquaintance with the spectacular abundance of colour provided by the more conventional mutliflowered cultivars seen and used by successful showmen.

Having determined and purchased your choice, the first year of growth will be largely one of diagnostic trial to ascertain the habit and potential of each plant. This is not necessarily a wasted season but one of fact finding for future cultural perfection if that is indeed your aim and intention. Many will of course collect and grow their plants principally for their own pleasure and satisfaction, placing more emphasis on multiformity of flower and growth within the species fuchsia.

Such collectors understandably get aggrieved over the limitation of choice presented to the public at various shows, but this is not too surprising considering all the known species, hybrids and cultivars in existence, many of which are of interest only to collectors and hybridists. Be that as it may, the range and diversity will attract many new enthusiasts and these will be best served by taking advantage of the many displays to be seen at botanical gardens such as Kew, Edinburgh or the RHS gardens at Wisley, Surrey, as well as the professional fuchsia nursery. All have some very interesting species, hybrids and cultivars not often seen at local shows.

Many species hybrids have become popular to a large number of enthusiasts and a brief description of some are given as an introduction to their distinctive charm. The most attractive and satisfying to grow must be the *triphylla* hybrids. Their beautiful foliage of dark bluish green or pale to olive green with variously suffused copper-bronze or purple-red underleaf must be seen to be fully appreciated. The flowers are borne in clusters and are quite distinctive, having long, slender tubes, short sepals and corollas of well-defined form. Colours range from deep red to orange-red and growth habit is strongly upright to arching. Well grown these excellent plants make good show plants. The natural variants of *F. fulgens* are also popular for show purposes and make very handsome and striking plants. The foliage is hirsute and light green to sage in colour, the individual leaf measuring some eight or nine inches. Flowers are long and are borne in pensile clusters, colours in shades of vermillion red with green tipped sepals, a truly noble plant that cannot fail to attract attention.

As a complete contrast and very attractive are the *breviflorae* hybrids. Most of these are of rampant growth, bearing diminutive flowers quite freely and solitary in the leaf axils. Colours range from varying shades of red to pinky white. The foliage is small and dainty giving the plant an overall fern-like appearance. They respond to good culture and will produce a shapely plant for the show bench. When acquainted with their charm they will surely command every grower's affection.

Other very satisfactory subjects for special attention are the various forms of *F. magellanica*, extremly graceful plants of slender arching growths producing what must be considered the most elegant and aesthetic of flower form, in colours of varying shades of red and mauve to purple. An alba form is available, as are forms with variegated foliage. They can be trained into many defined plant forms.

Some other of the species, not described here, will be of interest for many different reasons, and it is perhaps best that a personal selection be made from those offered in certain specialist fuchsia catalogues.

In preparing a list of fuchsia cultivars, one is immediately faced with a problem, not so much of what should be included, but of what one may leave out. It is thought that there are probably something in the region of 6,000 different cultivars that have at some time been recorded, though the number in present day cultivation is somewhat less than this.

Fuchsia Cultivars

There are of course many old varieties that still exist in private collections and on occasions one is privileged to see these. The list presented here, however, will be of plants that are easily obtainable, all of them being in general cultivation and having been selected and recommended because of their ease of growth, adaptability to a particular form of growth, suitability for show work, or because of a personal appreciation.

*Abbé Farges* French 1901. Semi-double; tube and sepals pale cerise; corolla lilac. Flowers small but very profuse. Growth upright and bushy, foliage small and sturdy. An excellent choice for small pot culture, but will also achieve larger dimensions if required and is often exhibited in 6 in pots.

*Achievement* British 1886. Single; tube and sepals cerise; corolla purple. Flowers medium to large, profuse and of good shape. The lightish green foliage is the perfect foil to beautiful flowers. Among one of the best British introductions, very easy to grow and will respond to any desired growth form.

*Alice Hoffman* German 1911. Semi-double; tube and sepals rose; corolla white, veined rose. Flowers small but numerous, foliage bronze overtones on green. Growth upright and bushy, ideal for small pot culture.

*Amelie Aubin* German 1884. Single; tube and sepals waxy white; corolla rose on cerise, white at base. Flowers large and of substantial quality and quantity. Growth pliant, requires frequent stopping to produce density for bush growth. This cultivar is worthy of every grower's time and attention.

*Athela* British 1942. Single, tube cream blushed pink, sepals damask pink, corolla salmon pink shading deeply at base. Flowers medium to large and produced freely. Growth responsive to early pinching back for a neat tidy bush form.

*Blue Elf* British 1968. Single; tube and sepals rose pink, corolla light blue shading deeper at edges, lightly veined pink. Flowers medium sized bell shaped. Foliage olive green with serrated edges. Growth upright and bushy. This cultivar won The Jones Cup at the BFS London Show for the Best New Introduction of the Year 1972.

*Bon Accorde* French 1861. Single; tube and sepals wax white; corolla pale purple on white. Flowers held high, an individual characteristic uniquely its own. Growth stiff and upright, needs an early encouragement to branch if a bush shape is required. Will make an excellent quarter standard and can be used for small pot culture.

*Bridesmaid* American 1952. Double; tube and sepals white blushed with carmine; corolla lilac deepening at outer edges. Flowers medium sized, very abundant and showy. Growth vigorous and responsive to chosen growth requirements. Medium sized heart-shaped foliage. This very lovely cultivar has a delicacy infinitely it's own and deserves to be rediscovered by the present day show enthusiasts.

*Brutus* French 1897. Single; tube and sepals rich red, corolla rich dark purple with slight red veining. Flowers medium sized and pro-duced freely. Growth upright and bushy. Everything about this plant spells vigour and health. As a showman's plant it must rank highly as it can be trained to almost any plant form definition.

*Carmel Blue* American 1956. Single, tube and sepals white with some virescence; sepals flushed delicate rose on underside tipped green; corolla dusky blue. Flowers medium sized and slimly elegant. Growth upright to arching. Early controlled growth provides for a shapely bush.

*Caroline* British 1967. Single, tube and sepals cream toned pink tipped light green; corolla cyclamen pink. Flowers large and flared, an attribute inherited from it's matriarchal parent Citation. Growth and foliage very similar but somewhat shorter jointed. Responds very well to bush training and makes an excellent fan or full standard.

*Cascade* American 1937. Single, tube and sepals white flushed carmine; corolla carmine. Flowers medium large and slender. Growth natural cascade, vigorous and self branching. Can be trained as pillar or standard but excels as a basket subject. Foliage and flowers are produced in great profusion but it is necessary to pay full attention to pinching back top growth to induce fullness and flower coverage to the crown.

*Celia Smedley* British 1970. Single; tube and sepals rose du Barry; corolla blood red. Flowers very freely produced. Growth is strong and lusty and will respond to almost any plant form definition. Without doubt this cultivar, by force of its colour impact and startling virility, has impressed every fuchsia pundit.

*Cloverdale Pearl* British 1974. Single; tube white; sepals pink to white tipped green, corolla white. Flowers very free and of medium size. Growth self branching and sturdy, an easy plant to train into a true bush as defined by BFS definition.

*Citation* American 1953. Single, tube and sepals rose pink; corolla white. Flowers are large and attractive, opening from companulate to perfect open saucer. Growth is upright and deceptively strong, holding its profusion of flower on slender wiry stems with an easy elegance. Well grown this cultivar will be the centre of attraction at any show.

*Countess of Aberdeen* British 1888. Single, tube and sepals very delicate pink, corolla white suffused pale pink. Flowers small but produced in clusters. Growth upright, short jointed and bushy. Needs little attention other than good growing conditions. Will bush naturally and strongly, and it makes an extremely attractive table standard.

*Dollar Princess* French 1912. Double, tube and sepals cerise, corolla rich purple. Flower medium to small but well formed. Growth vigorous and upright and will make an excellent bush. It can also be usefully employed as a low growing hedge. An easy cultivar suitable for the novice.

*Dorothea Flower* British 1969. Single, tube and sepals white, corolla soft violet blue. Flowers long and slenderly elegant, profuse. Growth willowy but wiry.

*Eleanor Leytham* British 1973. Single; tube and sepals white flushed pink; corolla pink with deeper pink edging. Flower small but profuse. Foliage thickly ribbed. Growth upright and bushy and rather stiff. Can make an excellent quarter standard but is a cultivar for the more experienced grower.

*Emile de Wildeman* (Synonymous with *Fascination*) French 1905. Double; tube and sepals rich red; corolla blush pink with rose intermixture and strong cerise veining. Flowers are fully double and profuse. Growth is strongly upright and free branching, requiring but little attention to produce a show plant.

*Flirtation Waltz* American 1962. Double; tube and sepals milk white flushed pink; corolla light rose. Flowers medium to large and attractively coquetish in full display. Growth vigorous and self branching bush. This cultivar will enrapture and delight all enthusiasts.

*Gladys Miller* British 1970. Single; tube and sepals cream overlaid pink tints; sepals spread outwards to terminate in wide angles and are tipped pale green; corolla pale lavender to lilac spreading from a white base. Foliage sharply serrated and abundant. This cultivar has a shrub growth and is naturally self branching, and will produce its flowers naturally for August shows. No stopping or pinching required, develops into a natural ball-shaped growth if left entirely to itself.

*Glitters* American 1963. Single; tube and sepals wax white inside of sepals reveal rich salmon hues; corolla glowing orange-red. Flowers are medium sized and produced profusely. Growth vigorous upright bush. Responds well to pinching.

*Golden Marinka* American 1955. Single; tube and sepals rich red; corolla a deeper red. Flowers medium sized and prolific. Foliage is very decorative and is perhaps its chief attraction. A show plant for basket cultivation, it is a natural trailer and is rarely used for any other purpose. A mutant of Marinka, it is less vigorous and versatile than its parent.

*Gruss aus dem Bodethal* German 1904. Tube and sepals richest crimson; corolla dark purple of such depth bordering black. Flowers small but produced freely. Growth somewhat tardy but bushes well.

Popular with every grower and exhibitor.

*Guinevere* American 1950. Single; tube and sepals white; corolla blue-violet. Flowers medium to large and free. Growth upright to arching, makes an excellent standard but usually grown as a bush, requires early pinching to encourage branching. This cultivar is one that really catches the eye and demands appreciation.

*Hawkeshead* British 1962. Single; tube and sepals white with distinct virescence, entire corolla white. Flowers classically beautiful in style, are shown to perfection against the dark green foliage. Growth upright and vigorous and bushy, an inspired piece of plant breeding.

*Heidi Ann* British 1969. Double; tube and sepals cerise; corolla lilac veined cerise. Flowers medium sized. Displays its fully double corolla to perfection if the plant is not pinched back too intensively, when they become small and tight. This cultivar is extremely popular on the show-bench. It flowers profusely and is tolerant of most growing conditions. A typical British cultivar, growth type is bush or half standard.

*Hilary* British 1970. Single; tube and sepals white flushed pink; corolla lavender overlaid darker tones at base. Flowers medium sized and prolific. Growth vigorous and upright, self branching.

*Iced Champagne* British 1968. Single; tube and sepals dawn pink; sepals tipped green; corolla rhodamine to blush pink. Flowers long, medium to large and of immaculate formation. Growth short jointed, bushy and neatly compact. A self branching cultivar that should be grown under cool conditions to obtain its full potential. This cultivar won The Jones Cup at the BFS London Show 1968.

*Jack Acland* American 1952. Single; tube and sepals pink; corolla deep rose pink. Flowers plentiful and of good substance. Growth upright and very bushy. Can be basket trained to huge dimensions or trained to a full standard. A well grown bush in full bloom cannot fail to impress. This cultivar has on occasions been confused with another of similar bloom named Jack Shahan: of the two cultivars it is our considered opinion that Jack Acland has more to offer in versatility of growth.

*Joy Patmore* British 1961. Single; tube and sepals alabaster white; corolla rich carmine paling slightly at base. Flowers medium sized produced severally at leaf axils ensuring constant flowering over long period. Growth upright compact bush. Conforms easily to any cultural form. This cultivar is another one that will excite attention by virtue of startling colour combination.

*Kings Ransome* American 1954. Double; tube and sepals translucent white; corolla rich deep purple. Flowers large and freely produced. Growth is strong upright and vigorous. An outstanding cultivar of show-bench quality. The blooms are extremely attractive and held well by the strong growth. Should be tried as a standard.

*La Campanella* British 1968. Semi-double; tube and sepals white with pink flush; corolla violet. Growth deceptive until established, then fills out in response to pinching. Flowers small and exceptionally prolific. Excels as a full or half-basket and will make an attractive quarter standard if so desired.

*Lady Isobel Barnet* British 1969. Single; tube and sepals rose red; corolla rose purple deepening to bishop purple at edges. Flowers are small to medium in size and displayed boldly to reveal an open type corolla, face up. Growth stiffly upright and will produce masses of bloom collectively. Excels as a bush and can be used for small pot culture with great success.

*Lady Kathleen Spence* British 1974. Single; tube and sepals white; amaranth-rose under sepals, which are long and narrow; corolla lavender to lilac. Flower medium sized and freely produced. Growth although upright and bushy has a rather frail appearance, very attractive and delicate. Will make a good basket and does well in a tub for the patio. This cultivar was awarded a Gold Certificate of Merit at the BFS Northern Show 1976.

*Lakeside* British 1967. Single; tube and sepals deep pink tipped green; corolla violet blue with pink veining. Flowers medium sized and extremely prolific. Growth is arcuate as opposed to lax. Responds to frequent stopping for bush growth and makes a beautiful cascading basket with good centre top growth, so essential in basket work.

*Lena Dalton* American 1953. Double; tube and sepals pale pink; corolla blue variegated rose. Flowers medium to large very free and distinctively showy. Growth upright and neatly bushy.

*Leonora* American 1960. Single; tube, sepals and corolla warm pink. Flowers medium sized with bell shaped corolla. The colour is clearly one of the best pinks to date and attracts all who see it. Growth is vigorous, upright and responds well to culture.

*Margharita* British 1970. Double; tube and sepals soft pink, corolla white. Flowers large, perfectly formed and sound of texture. Growth robust upright and bushy. Produces massive growth and flower as a second-year plant.

*Marin Glow* American 1954. Single; tube and sepals paper white; corolla rich imperial purple. Flowers medium sized and very profuse. The stark colour combination fascinates the attention of all eyes making it a showman's *pièce de résistance*. Growth upright, strong and bushy.

*Marinka* French 1902. Single; tube and sepals rich red; corolla a deeper red. Flowers medium sized and extremely profuse. Growth strong and cascading. Makes an excellent pyramid over two seasons of cultural attention. This cultivar is, however, constantly used with overwhelming regularity for basket work and is rarely surpassed for sheer mass of bloom overall.

*Melody* American 1942. Single; tube and sepals rose pink; corolla cyclamen purple. Flowers are medium sized and plentiful. Growth vigorous and free branching, excellent for standards or columns and ideal for bush and shrub culture.

*Mieke Meursing* British 1968. Semi-double; tube and sepals red; corolla a somewhat murky pink. Flowers medium sized and are produced in great profusion, often to a point of being overcrowded. Growth is similarly boisterous and freely branching with auxiliary growth springing from the root system, adding to the overall density. This cultivar stormed its way on to the show benches for several years but is now strangely less popular among top growers. However it is a marvellous plant and will be valued by all who possess it.

*Ming* British 1968. Single; tube and sepals orange red; corolla cherry red. Flowers small with short stubby tubes firmly constructed, having an eastern aura about them, possibly emanating from glowing colour combination. Growth upright and vigorous. Good as outside bedder.

*Mission Bells* American 1948. Single; tube and sepals scarlet; corolla rich purple. Flowers medium to large and bell shaped. Growth upright, a vigorous bush, producing its flowers freely. A great favourite of many long-standing exhibitors.

*Mrs Marshall* British (date unknown). Single; tube and sepals ivory white suffused rose blush on sepals; corolla rosy cerise. Flowers medium sized and freely produced. Growth upright, strong and free branching. Ideal for pyramid or other large specimens.

*Mrs W. Rundle* British 1883. Single; tube and sepals are a waxy pale rose; corolla glowing orange vermillion. Flowers large and long, produced freely. The foliage is large and light green complimenting the graceful flowers perfectly. Needs some support as a bush growth and requires early pinching to encourage laterals. Should make a good weeping standard or basket growth if desired.

*Pacquesa* British 1974. Single; tube and sepals deep red; corolla intense white lightly veined at base. Flowers large, firm and of great substance, produced freely. Growth strong upright and bushy with attractive foliage. A good solid plant in every way.

*Pat Meara* British 1962. Single; tube and sepals rose pink; corolla veronica blue spreading from white central band. Flowers medium to large and are fully flared and produced very freely. Growth upright and vigorous. This cultivar won The Jones Cup at the BFS Show London 1962.

*Phyllis* British 1938. Semi-double; tube and sepals roseate flushed cerise; corolla deep rose. Flowers small but very profuse, growth upright and very vigorous. Will develop half standards in one season and can be used for pyramid, column, bush, shrub and espalier. A very worthwhile and versatile cultivar for every beginner.

*Royal Velvet* American 1962. Double; tube and sepals bright crimson; corolla purple streaked crimson from base. Flowers are produced freely for such large blooms. Growth is strong and vigorous. Controlled pinching back assures a well branched and floriferous bush needing little, if any support.

*Sleigh Bells* American 1954. Single; tube and sepals white, the sepals are long and thin tipped light green; the corolla on newly opened flowers appear tubular, later opening to a perfect bell shape. Growth upright and free branching, will make a very good standard.

*Snowcap* British (date unknown). Semi-double, tube and sepals bright red; corolla intense white faintly veined red. Flowers are borne profusely and freely. Growth upright and strong, self branching. Ideally suited for pyramid, conical or bush. Requires a minimum of cultural effort to produce a showy plant.

*Swanley Gem* British 1901. Single; tube and sepals rich scarlet; corolla deep violet blue veined scarlet. Flowers of medium size, petals open flat saucer shaped into a perfect circle. Growth upright and bushy, always attracts attention wherever shown.

*Swingtime* American 1950. Double; tube and sepals rich red of a crepe texture; corolla light ivory, faintly veined pink at base. Flowers of good size and free. Growth upright and free branching. An adaptable plant, it will adjust to any training. A show plant of great distinction.

*Sunray* British 1872. Single; tube and sepals cerise; corolla carmine. Flower small. This cultivar is listed here not so much for its bloom but for its most attractive foliage displayed handsomely on a splendid plant this is both vigorous and shapely. The foliage has an indefinite amount of light green and pale cream markings both of which have casts of cerise becoming more intense as the leaves develop. It is best treated as a greenhouse subject and given full light.

*Tennessee Waltz* American 1951. Semi-double; tube and sepals rose madder; corolla lilac lavender flushed rose. Medium sized flower of squarish shape has upswept sepals, flowers very freely produced. A self branching plant of strong upright growth, an ideal plant for the beginner. Will make an excellent bush or standard.

*Ting a Ling* American 1959. Single; tube and sepals and corolla white. Flowers medium to large. The corolla opens out more bowl than saucer shaped and is inclined to pink slightly if given full sunshine. Growth is strongly upright and free branching. This cultivar is without doubt the connoisseurs' choice of an all white fuchsia and needs greenhouse space and protection if show bench perfection is desired.

*Tom Thumb* French 1860. Single; tube and sepals carmine red; corolla mauve veined red. Small flower freely produced. Ideal for small pot culture and rockeries, growth upright and bushy.

*The Aristocrat* American 1953. Double; tube creamy white; sepals are upswept pale rose tipped white; corolla creamy white veined pale rose. Flower large and well formed with serrated petals of solid substance. Growth vigorous and upright, a really lovely bloom of classic form.

Ornamental and Variegated Foliage Cultivars

This type of cultivar is becoming more popular for use on the show bench, so much so, that most show schedules now include separate classes for these delightful and handsome plants. Unfortunately they are not catered for in the British Fuchsia Society's *Handbook of Plant Form Definition and Judging Criteria*, so that some guidance may be helpful.

The definition of a variegated leaf is one that exhibits two or more distinct colours and is quite straightforward. This is not so with the definition of ornamental, which means in this sense a plant grown for its beauty, or more precisely, for the beauty of its leaves, which is rather vague for both the judge as well as the exhibitor.

Cultivars that display a light green leaf are the real problem plants because many that fall into this category have leaves that darken with age and cannot really be classed as ornamental. Plants with leaves that are distinctly yellow, usually described as golden, particularly if accompanied with red veining in the leaf, are a much better proposition and less likely to be marked NAS.

Plants exhibited in this type of class should be grown in accordance with one of the recognised plant form definitions, although it may be found that some of these cultivars are not quite as free flowering as one would wish. However, this is usually allowed for in the judges' assessment as the foliage is of prime importance. This can be achieved by ensuring that the plant enjoys a good light intensity and by following the usual cultural procedures, but care must be taken with overhead watering, which will mark the foliage.

Because of the problems that may be experienced in choosing suitable ornamental cultivars for show purposes, a selection of these together with a few of the better variegated leaved cultivars are described here separately.

*Autumnale* (Synonymous with *Burning Bush* and *Rubens*). The name Autumnale is widely used and accepted in this country, contrary to what is now considered to be the correct name, Rubens. It is thought that the plant was introduced in the late eighteenth century, subsequently lost to cultivation but rediscovered in Europe, later to be sent out from two difference sources, each bearing different names. Burning Bush would appear to be the first on the scene, but it was not until 1930 when sent out as autumnale that this cultivar captured general acclaim and acceptance of name. The single flowers are medium sized, tube and sepals scarlet, corolla purple. Growth is stiffly spreading, at times laterals are horizontal to main stem. Foliage coloration changes through green and yellow to autumnale tints of gold, to rich mahogany and russet.

*Candy Rose* American 1964. Double; tube and sepals red and of a crepe texture; corolla pale pink with deep pink variegation. Flower medium sized, foliage bronze-green on an upright and bushy growth.

*Carl Drude* British 1975. Semi-double; tube and sepals cardinal red; corolla white veined red. Flower of medium size but very free. Foliage golden-bronze. An upright and bushy growth.

*Cloth of Gold* British 1863. Single; tube and sepals red; corolla purple. A medium sized flower though not very abundant. Foliage is golden but ages to darkish green flushed bronze with rose casts on underside.

*Day by Day* British 1971. Single; tube and sepals scarlet; corolla rosy-purple. Foliage marbled green, cream and cerise. Growth is bushy.

*Dominyana* British 1852. Single; a rich scarlet self. A long trumpet-shaped tube and small sepals. Foliage a deep bronze-purple. Flowers are borne in terminal clusters.

*Dunrobin Castle* British (date unknown). A variant of *F. magellanica var. globosa*. Tube and sepals scarlet; corolla purple. Flower small. Foliage is a bright green and coral combination.

*Firefall* American 1939. Single; tube and sepals clear carmine; corolla a warmer shade of carmine. Medium-sized flower, freely produced. Foliage a glowing red-bronze.

*Geneii* American 1961. Single; tube and sepals cerise; corolla rich violet. Flower small but very free. Foliage small, a bright yellowish-green on red stems, some red veining in leaf. Growth upright and buhsy.

*Gilda* British 1971. Double; tube and sepals coral; corolla coral, over-laid rose blush with petal edges distinctly outlined bright red. Flowers large and produced freely. Foliage golden-green with maroon coloration. Growth upright to arching.

*Golden Gate* American 1940. Single; tube and sepals red; corolla rich purple. Flower small but free. Foliage bright golden-yellow. Growth compact, dense and bushy.

*Golden Glory* American 1970. Double; tube and sepals orange tones; corolla of similar but clearer colouring, almost a self. Flower medium and free. Foliage golden, commencing red at leaf base.

*Golden Marinka* (previously described under cultivars p. 54).

*Golden Treasure* British 1860. Single; tube and sepals scarlet; corolla purple-magenta. Flowers small and rather sparse. A most attractive foliage, having variegated green and gold markings with red veining. Growth is a spreading bush.

*Potney's Tricolour* British 1842. Single; tube and sepals red; corolla blush-purple. Flower small. Foliage marbled green and white, suffused overall with bright pink. Requires full sunshine. Upright growth.

*Sunray* (Previously described under cultivars p. 59).

*Tricolorii* (Described under hardy cultivars p. 123).

*Tropic Sunset* American 1965. Double; tube and sepals carmine; corolla deep purple with pink splashes. Flowers small and free. Foliage rather small, reddy-bronze with greenish tips. A self branching trailing cultivar with red stems.

*Wave of Life* British 1869. Single; tube and sepals scarlet; corolla red-purple. Flower small and free. Foliage golden-green. Stiff spreading bush.

The *Triphylla* Hybrids

The range of flower colour within this group of hybrids is perhaps not very wide in the true sense, but all the shades or pigments of red to orange are there with striking intensity. The flowers are borne in abundant terminal clusters, and all carry the distinctive long tube, short sepals and corollas, received by descent from *F. triphylla*, the first recorded species.

Unfortunately these hybrids cannot survive frost or low temperatures and will require an overwintering temperature of at least 40°F (5°C). This is well within the scope of most greenhouse owners and all should take advantage of it to grow these most beautiful and attractive of fuchsias.

For most enthusiasts it is the foliage that intrigues and fascinates most of all, for there on the reverse of varying shades of green velvety textured leaves are revealed subtle hues of bronze, copper, red, purple and blue.

Typical growth is mostly upright to arching and will usually benefit from an early pinch to encourage low growth and production of a well shaped bush or shrub. Others have been developed but not too successfully as show specimens.

The following list is a selection of easily obtainable plants from specialist fuchsia nurserymen:

*Andenken an Heinrich Henkel* Tube very long, light crimson flushed faintly cinnabar; sepals rose; corolla deep salmon. Foliage dark green flushed purple-red. Growth loosely upright.

*Billy Green* Long tubed salmon-pink self. Foliage olive green. Growth upright and vigorous. The flowers are borne in great profusion over the entire plant making it probably the finest show plant within the group.

*Gartenmeister Bonstedt* Long tubed glowing orange-red self. Foliage dark bronze-red. Growth very vigorous and upright, will bloom freely and continuously if given protection.

*Koralle (Coralle)* Long tubed salmon-orange self; foliage, deep blue-green velvety leaves. Growth vigorous and upright, requires some shade against direct sunshine.

*Mantilla* Long tubed rich carmine-red self. Sepals and corolla very small. Foliage bronze-green. Growth lax to cascade.

*Mary* Long tubed vivid scarlet-red self. Flowers freely, foliage narrow, blue-green veined magenta, reverse of leaf purple. Growth upright to arching.

*Stella Ann* Long tubed, brilliant red; sepals coral tipped green; corolla burnt orange; very free flowering. Foliage olive green, reverse of leaf deep blush. Growth upright and bushy.

*Thalia* Long tubed orange-scarlet self, small sepals and corolla. Extremely free flowering, foliage dark olive green with pronounced magenta veining, some bronzing on the leaf is also evident. Growth is extremely vigorous and upright. Its habit of growth and continuous flowering, quite apart from its show bench qualities, makes this the most popular of all bedding out plants.

*Traudchen Bonstedt* Long tubed pale salmon pink self. Foliage light green flushed bronze. Reverse of leaf tinted red. Growth upright, flowers freely.

*Trumpeter* Long tubed, bright geranium-lake self. Foliage dark blue-green, growth lax to cascade, free flowering.

# CHAPTER 5

# Defined Plant Forms

Whether one grows fuchsias for exhibition or not, a well grown and well flowered plant is the ultimate objective of most growers. The fuchsia lends itself to many shapes and may be trained in more ways possibly than any other plant. It can be trained and grown in the roof of a greenhouse, or in hanging and wall baskets when it will show off its blooms to perfection. The variety of shapes that can be grown in pots is almost endless, from the popular bush and shrub shape, the varying heights of the standard forms, through the conical, pyramid and pillar, conjuring visions of stately grandeur, to the more manageable espalier and fan shapes.

An Introduction to Training

With care and winter protection these larger specimen plants will grow in stature over the years, as proved by the legendary standards of Marinka at Mill Hill School. These famous plants were reputed to be well over 50 years old and still each year gave a very creditable show of flower.

Many exhibitors show plants that are two to three years old, but it is quite possible to produce a plant of exhibition quality entirely from the current year's growth. Hanging baskets, bush, ball, shrub and quarter standards are quite easily produced from cuttings rooted in mid-winter. These young plants although suffering from low light levels at this time of the year, are nevertheless growing and producing good root systems and will be in an advanced state of development by the mid-spring. This is achieved by encouraging lateral growth on the plant in its earlier stages of development (this will also apply to quarter standards once the head section is commenced). The more stops that are made, the greater the number of laterals and, eventually, flowering tips that are achieved, an essential requisit of the present-day show fuchsia.

In one season only a limited number of stops are possible if the plant is to flower at a given time. Therefore, if the plant is being trained for exhibition, the timing of flower production is of the upmost importance, as it should be at its peak of flowering perfection on the day of the show.

Many plants may, however, lose weeks of growth if the growing tip should be allowed to develop too much before removal. This causes an accumulated delay to successive stops and could well deprive the grower of the opportunity of a further stop which could have doubled the flowering mass.

A little delicacy is required of course, but young growing tips can be snapped off quite easily when very small by applying a slight pressure to one side of the growth. It is essential that the plant is in a turgid condition before this is attempted and a wise precaution is to make sure that plants are watered at least an hour before any stops are made.

The considerate grower will never combine the two operations of potting and stopping, as each operation will be a slight check to the plant's growth. Of the two, potting should take precedence.

For show purposes a preference for first-year plants is advocated where possible. Of course full standards, pillars and conicals are not possible in one season of growth, but plants that can be produced on this system have a distinct advantage over older plants in that they have a suppleness and more youthful quality about them that can never be recaptured by their more mature counterparts, however well groomed and presented.

But to propose that all other methods of culture are entirely without merit or consideration would be misleading and deny the cultural trend among many growers, who have developed a biennial plant system that yields a greater quantity of growth for plants restricted to a 6 in maximum pot size. These plants are not simply second-year plants as such, but products of a disciplined, planned cultural programme through one season to another.

The most popular form of plant growth exhibited is the shrub, but the biennial system is adaptable to the bush and espalier forms, although the latter will demand more attention to plant form requirements.

Cuttings rooted and established in thumb pots by early April are calculated to give a short season of development, sufficient to complete the first stage of basic structure to a final pot size of 4-4½ in maximum. As development progresses, a favourable position in the open air, shaded against strong sunlight, must be provided to prevent rapid drying out and premature hardening of wood.

Every aid to promote good growth is and will be a crucial test of ability and dedication. Routine feeding and watering as required is critical during high season when the plants should be given cooling overhead sprays as often as possible to create that congenial atmosphere so conducive to robust growth.

Some crowding of roots can be expected with the more vigorous types towards the end of the season, but by that time growth will be slowing down and a period of rest should be encouraged at the beginning of Autumn even if the plant is still in flower. A gradual withholding of water will advance the process of rest to complete dormancy and loss of foliage, at which stage the plants can be stored on their sides in the cold but frost free greenhouse. Occasional inspection is advisable and prudent to assure all is well. Never allow complete drying out of the plant soil and equally important, avoid conditions that promote premature re-growth. A light pruning aligned to shape requirements can be undertaken when growth buds develop sufficiently to herald the next season of active growth. Re-potting, fully explained elsewhere, can be delayed until growth is under way.

Exercise great care and pot back into the smallest practical size. This can be helped by teasing out as much of the old soil as possible from the root system before placing into the smaller pot. Water the plant well and provide the finest growing conditions possible.

It will be obvious that the plant has suffered a setback, but given a week or two, new roots will have been layed down and a balanced root system and shoot development will quickly adjust.

When the plants are once again growing freely, the gradual multiplication of lateral growths, achieved through constant stopping, must be trained and cared for by giving particular attention to future cultural procedures. The plants must never be allowed to suffer checks in their continuous growth at any time, and watering and potting-on must be attended to with some diligence.

A dilute liquid feed can be given during the period of rapid growth between potting successions, but must only be used as an inducement to sustain vigour until the next potting-on is carried out.

The use of cane supports as an aid to shape arrangement is a matter of anticipation and foresight. Such supports should be placed in position at a time when further growths can develop around them to conceal their presence.

The final stage of vegetative growth and eventual flower production is supported principally by skilful management to overcome the consequences of root restraint and soil exhaustion. At this stage supplementary feeding in association with frequent watering must be programmed and sustained.

It is necessary to shade against excessive exposure to strong sunshine and spray overhead frequently during particularly hot weather to alleviate any stress caused by rapid respiration. Overhead spraying should of course cease when flower buds begin to show colour, but the staging or standing ground can be well watered to provide humidity.

67

Most who begin to grow fuchsias for the show bench are faced with the problem of not knowing which cultivars are the most suitable for a particular type of shape, and very often their earlier efforts are spoilt by no more than an incorrect selection of cultivar for the shape they wish to achieve. An interesting experiment that can quite easily be undertaken with a plant of which they have no experience, is to root a cutting in the normal way and just grow it on one stem, potting-on as required. A cane should be provided at an early stage and the central stem should be tied in as growth develops. The plant should not be stopped at any time and should be allowed to flower in its own time. Many points of growth habit can be discovered about a plant grown in this manner.

If the beginner starts a plant as early in the season as possible and keeps potting on until a size 9 in pot is reached, by which time the plant will want to flower, almost everything that can be known about the plant's habit and suitability for a particular shape will be there for observation. After the various points have been noted, it may well be found that the plant can be grown on the following year either as a standard or a pillar, providing some attempt is made to train to the chosen shape before the end of the first season.

## Training Shrubs

For many reasons this plant form is the most popular type cultivated. It is ideal for the garden and is also the subject of intense competition on the show bench. Recently re-classified by the BFS for show purposes it was previously grouped with the bush. There are numerous cultivars suitable for shrub growth, all of which have the ability to throw up auxiliary shoots from the root system.

As with all plant forms, good culture starts with a well rooted cutting. The value of the small tip cutting quickly rooted is very well illustrated here, where lateral and auxiliary root shoots must be encouraged with an early stop. The frequency or infrequency of stopping the plant to produce further side growth is a decision that individual growers must take. Much will depend on the vigour and habit of growth of the chosen cultivar, or a personal liking of growth style, be it the loose open effect or the more controlled compact growth. Both styles are accepted on equal merit but the choice of style must be in agreement with and suitable to the plant itself, whichever style is decided upon. Generally the short jointed cultivars are the more suitable for compact controlled growth style.

The timing of the last stop before flower production cannot be exact, and is to a great extent a matter of general anticipation based on experience. After the last stop is made, the plant will have received quite a severe check (with the short jointed cultivar there may have been something in the region of 60 tips removed) so the plant should be allowed a day or two to recover and then be given a feed of nitrogenous fertiliser to promote production of side shoots. These shoots will eventually become flowering stems, making possibly three or four pairs of leaves before initiation of flower buds. It is often stated that single flowered cultivars require six weeks from the last stop to flower production. With a few cultivars this might be possible, and most will show the odd flower at this stage, but it will be found that eight weeks will be much more appropriate for the single flowered cultivars and ten weeks should be allowed for the double flowered plants.

The practice followed by many growers after the last stop, is to feed their plants with a high concentration of potash to promote flowering. This practice is not to be recommended, as its overall effect is all too often to create plants with small flowers, and small brittle leaves on a framework of hard and woody branches, at a time when the plant should be at perfection. To keep the record straight, it must be said again that an increase of potassium is required at this time to ensure a good production of flower, but this must be accompanied by the presence of adequate supplies of phosphorus and nitrogen.

Potassium when fed to a plant continuously over a period of 2-2½ months (from the last stop to flowering) can do two things: it can restrict the action of available nitrogen and also probably induce a magnesium deficiency, which in turn affects the mobility of phosphorus. Therefore the supplementary feeding, after the last stop has been made, must include nitrogen, phosphorus and potassium. It is recommended that they should be applied in a ratio of 1:1:2.

## Bush

The recently revised Judging Standard of the BFS requires that the bush form is developed so that a short stem, free of all growth, to a maximum of 1½ in, can be seen, to indicate that the plant is constructed from a single cultivar. Therefore all growth must emanate from a selected number of laterals from which the bush shape is formed.

Auxiliary shoots springing from below the soil surface must not be allowed to develop and should be removed as soon as possible. This will allow all growth energy to be concentrated on the development of the bush itself and will give the grower complete control of cultural direction.

Early consideration must be given to the establishment of the short stem, the length of which must take into account any subsequent potting with the consequent lowering of the soil ball together with future mulches to the soil surface, if a clear stem is to be observed.

Again, one's personal choice of growth style will to a certain extent dictate the choice of cultivar to be used and, if one's preference is for the open type of growth, the length of stem between leaves is perhaps not quite so critical but if a more compact style is required then the short jointed cultivar is indicated.

Cuttings when rooted should be potted into the smallest size pot and should be allowed to develop four or five pairs of leaves. If during this time the plant requires repotting, this should on no account be delayed whatever the size of the plant. When the required number of pairs of leaves has developed the plant must be stopped to initiate the production of side growths. The top four resulting laterals are then chosen as the basic framework on which to build-up the subsequent shape. All growths below the required laterals must be removed to establish the clear stem.

When selecting the lateral growths on which to build the structure it may be that four, which has been suggested, may not be sufficient. Much will in fact depend on the chosen cultivar, as with some it could be that six will be a better proposition and experience and knowledge of the cultivar will be the final deciding factor.

The laterals are allowed to develop two pairs of leaves and are then stopped, the process being repeated with subsequent laterals until such time as the whole plant has reached the stage when the ultimate shape modifies the stopping programme, and stopping is then entirely concerned with shaping the plant as opposed to building up the density of the structure. Once the shape has been achieved, stopping continues until ten weeks (for double flowered cultivars) and, eight weeks (for the single flowered cultivars) before the required flowering period.

During this building-up process the plant must be potted-on as often as the root system demands and, to this end, the root system must be inspected every week to ten days from the previous potting to ensure that the plant is in no way becoming 'pot bound'. If the plant is intended for show work the potting-on should continue until the time when the size of pot is reached that is required by the show schedule. From now on the plant will not have the benefit of fresh compost being added and the roots will become restricted in their outward growth, tending to wind themselves round the soil-ball so that the whole pot becomes a mass of roots. This, to a certain extent, at this stage is necessary as it helps to encourage flowering, but until such time as flowers are required the root mass must be provided with ample supplies of water, and the fertiliser should not have any increase in potash until all stopping is completed.

It is the nature of plant growth to reproduce itself and, in a natural environment, this follows an ordered pattern dictated by seasonal change. However when grown under artificial conditions,

70

it is of the utmost importance to provide the correct conditions for the stage of growth required by the grower at a particular time. Thus if a plant is allowed to remain in a dry condition when the pot is full of roots, it is almost bound to initiate flower buds as the first stage of the reproductive cycle.

At the stage when the pot is full of roots, feeding is also very important, since the continual watering demanded by the plant, particularly during hot weather, will leach out fertilisers from the compost and these must of course be replaced at frequent intervals to ensure the well being of the plant. To equalise plant growth it is essential to turn the plant at least two or three times a week so that all parts of the plant enjoy the benefit of an equal amount of time facing the strongest light source. Failure to do this will result in an asymmetrical plant structure.

Ball

The ball form of growth is in many ways similar in cultivation to that of both the bush and shrub and when well grown and correctly shaped should appear, as its name suggests, like a ball. This effect is achieved by meticulous attention to training the lateral growths of the selected cultivar which should be of an arching type growth habit, free branching, fairly vigorous and short jointed, the latter being required to produce the density and compactness so important to creating the correct effect.

When properly trained the lateral growths of the ball should arch over and down, completely encompassing the container with the tips of the laterals just brushing the surface on which the container stands.

The young cutting is stopped at two pairs of leaves to encourage a dense growth from the outset. Thereafter lateral growth in the centre of the structure must be stopped more frequently than the outer growths which are trained to grow gradually downward, this action in itself inducing fullness to the ball shape by stimulating further lateral growths near the bends. These in turn are stopped, to coincide with either the shape required at this point, or, are allowed to grow on and become further long laterals arching over the container. Weight strings can be usefully employed to train strong growths to arch over in the required position. When the required shape has been achieved, stopping and timing for flower production will be as for other types.

Any training media used must be removed for show purposes and it is expected that the container will be obscured by a neat ball of leaf and flower over the entire body of the plant.

## Hanging Baskets

One of the most popular ways of displaying fuchsias is in hanging baskets and wall baskets, both being used extensively for decorating patios, loggias, etc., as well as being very popular for exhibition work. There are many cultivars suitable for basket culture, although some are better than others, and should a basket be intended for exhibition work it is advisable not to use cultivars of a very lax growth habit as they do not produce the overall effect required for exhibition purposes.

The regulation maximum size of a basket intended for exhibition is 15in in diameter, which when planted and at its flowering peak can measure 30 in or more in diameter. Plants of lax habit will never achieve these proportions, added to which there is a tendency for this type of cultivar to produce most of the flower at the lower ends of the growths, leaving the top of the basket almost bereft of blooms. Good cultivation can do little to improve this state of affairs and it is therefore advisable to select cultivars that have an arching type of growth habit and, experience will show that these will produce the better effect.

Over many years, Marinka and its mutation Golden Marinka, have proved themselves ideal types for hanging baskets and are the perfect plants for the newcomer to exercise his or her skill on before experimenting with the many other suitable cultivars available. Of course one's own particular favourite can be tried and may well prove successfull providing the growth habit is not too lax or too stiffly upright.

Having selected the correct type of cultivar, five or six cuttings should be rooted in the normal way, and potted into a pot size 3 in maximum. They can be given their first stop after two pairs of leaves have formed. There is no need for a cane support and in fact they may be encouraged to trail over the edge of the pot.

Young plants should not be allowed to become pot-bound and as soon as roots have penetrated the side of the root ball and are beginning to move down the side of the pot they are ready to be moved into the basket.

When planting the basket it will be found that the most convenient way will be to sit the basket on top of a 9 in pot or some other similar recepticle to hold it steady while working. The first step is to line the basket with florist or sphagnum moss. This should be spread over the whole of the inside and trimmed off with scissors at the top edge. For some years now it has been the practice of many growers to put a second liner of thin-gauge polythene on top of the moss to help retain the compost and to a certain extent moisture. If it should be found that this is necessary because the layer of moss is not sufficient to retain the compost properly throughout the season, it might well be found that a better second liner can be made with old discarded nylon stockings or tights. These may be cut into pieces of suitable size and will be much more manageable than a polythene liner and less noticeable in the finished product. Whichever the choice for the inner liner it is advisable to use one or the other, as baskets do tend to dry out quickly in hot weather and are consequently subjected to frequent and liberal watering and this, if the moss liner is on the thin side, will result over a period of time, in much of the compost being washed out. If polythene is used, it must be punctured to allow any excess water to drain away, but this problem will not arise if the nylon is used.

At this point, and particularly if the basket is to be used for exhibition do not, as is becoming the practice, dispense with the moss entirely, because if the trailing growths do not come well below the bottom of the basket, or until such time as they do, nothing offends the eye more than the lack of moss or the sight of crumpled polythene of lurid colour.

The cost of sphagnum moss, like so many other items, is becoming high, and the temptation not to use it is appreciated, but it should be remembered that in competition it is not only the plants that are appraised, but presentation is also taken into account and consideration.

The next step is partially to fill the basket with compost and this should be spread up the sides as far as possible, creating a saucer effect, and into this are placed four or five plants at equidistant intervals around the edge and at a slight outward angle with the growth laying over the side of the basket. Compost is then worked into the spaces between the soil balls while leaving a space in the centre for another plant. This centre plant should, if possible, be somewhat larger than the others as it will help to fill out the middle more fully. Further compost is now added until the whole basket is filled and the surface is finished off with a slight depression towards the centre to help prevent water from flowing over the sides.

Once the basket is planted and placed into its position it is essential that it is kept well watered, and a regular feeding programme must be maintained as plants in baskets do not get the benefit of potting-on and the consequent addition of fresh compost.

Stopping the growths in basket culture is perhaps not quite so intensive as with some other forms but must still be attended to with some diligence. Once the growth has come over the edge of the basket it should only be stopped sufficiently to give an even distribution of trailing growths of a density to completely hide the basket, and when this is achieved the trailing laterals should be allowed to develop length. That part of the plant which is situated over the top of the basket should be stopped in much the same way as one would for a compact bush, that is, at every pair of leaves until such time as the whole top of the basket is covered. These laterals are then in turn allowed to grow and develop length and should be trained to blend in with those resulting from the plants originally placed around the edge of the basket. It may seem that one is growing on two systems and in the early stages this is in fact what is happening. The larger centre plant must be trained initially to grow up to add height and density to the middle of the basket after which the laterals arch over and blend in with those below, at which point the whole basket is treated as one unit.

### Wall Baskets

For wall baskets training and culture is very similar to that for full baskets, although more emphasis on top growth is necessary as the wall basket is often at a lower level with the top more in view. An arching cascade of trailing growth of sufficient density to cover the top, front and sides of the basket should be aimed for. Feeding and watering are essential to good culture and must never be overlooked. If stems are allowed to collapse from lack of water they rarely recover completely, especially if full of flower.

## Standards

This type of growth form is really only practical for the greenhouse owner, if the larger specimens are to be constructed, as it is usual for the first season to be devoted to developing a strong straight stem or trunk and the commencement of the flowering head. It is rarely possible to produce a full standard in one season even when using the most vigorous of cultivars. The second season will achieve the full size of head, developing a depth and diameter in proportion to its overall height.

For show purposes, the BFS requirement for a full standard is a length of clear stem of not less than 30 in and not more than 42 in, from soil level to the first break.

A well-rooted cutting with a potential for strong vigorous growth should be selected and potted into a pot size that will just accommodate the root system comfortably. A split cane is inserted, as near to the stem of the plant as possible, care being taken not to damage the young root system, and a tie should be made as low as possible to the cane. Support for the young plant is essential at this stage and any deviation from the upright must be avoided by frequent ties as growth extension of the stem proceeds. The directional pull of light, or 'phototropic' effect, is very strong and once a curvature is established correction is rarely possible.

At this stage growth is entirely concentrated on building a strong trunk. Leaves must be retained to assist in the process of enlarging the diameter of the trunk; early laterals may also be retained, but should be removed before they affect the clean line of the trunk, for if left to develop too well they often leave a pronounced lump at the nodes.

Particular attention must be made to potting requirements. It is very important that no overcrowding of roots occurs, as this can result in hard wood and an inducement to flower. Roots should therefore be inspected frequently and, as soon as they appear through the side of the root ball, the plant moved to the next size pot.

When repotting plants that are required to produce fast, vigorous growth they should always be potted-on before the roots emerging from the side of the root ball reach the bottom of the pot. Failure to re-pot in good time will allow the roots to wind round the root ball and commence the 'pot habit'. If this is allowed to proceed unchecked it will be almost impossible for the roots to penetrate the fresh soil in any future pottings.

As growth proceeds, the development of the head section must be attended to. The number of laterals required for this is dependent to a great extent on trunk length, an important feature of a good standard being balance, that is, the depth of head in relation to diameter and length of stem. This is usually considered to be a depth of head one third of the total height, with the diameter of head in proportion to the depth. These measurements can only be an approximation and the grower will with experience develop his or her own individual style. Full weeping standards with a depth of head half the total height of the plant look delightful but are rarely seen these days in competition on the show bench.

Once the total height is reached, i.e. 30 in of clear stem plus the section allowed for the depth of head, the top must be taken out and, if they have not already been removed, all the side shoots up to the first break must be taken away. However, the leaves must still be retained on the trunk at this time. The resulting lateral growth in the head section is allowed to develop and the first stop made is dependent on the type of cultivar being used. It is impossible to state categorically that this should be done at two or three pairs of leaves, as much will depend on the length of joint between the pairs of leaves. One should be very conscious at this stage of the eventual diameter and density of the head required, and should attempt to visualise the number of stops possible to obtain the desired size and shape in the finished product.

The stopping of laterals and subsequent side shoots continues, gradually building up the head, and this is coupled with a regular feeding programme of a balanced fertiliser. When the laterals have been stopped twice, all the leaves up to the first break should be removed together with any secondary development of side growths, to ensure a good clean stem.

Many growers when selecting cutting material that is intended to be used for growing standards try to use the tips of stems that have leaves in whorls of three (see Figure 5.1). These when rooted will produce three side shoots at each node instead of the usual two, thereby increasing the density of the head section more quickly.

Figure 5.1
Stem showing
Leaves in
Whorls of Three

The half standard is probably the more popular form grown by the amateur, being somewhat more manageable and rather quicker in reaching maturity than the full standard. Culture is the same as for the standard form and, again the vigorous cultivar should be selected. With the very fast growing types, for example, Phyllis and Joan Smith, a fair sized head can be achieved in one season. Attention to potting and feeding must be regularly attended to, to prevent any check in the rate of growth. The trunk length is really the only difference from the full standard and the depth of head and the diameter should again be in proportion to the total height.

**Half Standards**

When selecting cultivars for the half standard form, apart from vigour, the size of flower is a point that needs to be considered. It is advisable to use cultivars with medium sized blooms as the very large flowered types are often rather sparsely flowered.

Half standards should have a stem length of not less than 18 in and not more than 30 in if they are to be used for competition on the show bench.

Without doubt the quarter or table standard is the most popular of all the standard forms and there are many enchanting cultivars that can grow and flower in one season. They are much more convenient for the small greenhouse owner and most novice growers test their skill growing these before attempting the larger forms described above. Cultivation is the same as for the larger types of standard but the quarter standard matures more quickly.

**Quarter Standards**

The vigour of the selected cultivar for this type of growth is perhaps not quite so essential but the stem needs to be run up in time to develop the head sufficiently for a reasonable flowering season.

Quarter standards when well cultivated have neat, compact, dense head sections. This is achieved by using short jointed, small flowered cultivars which are stopped at two pairs of leaves throughout the building up process.

The length of clear stem should not be less than 12 in and not more than 18 in from soil level to the first break. It may be found with quarter standards, that by leaving the pair of leaves immediately below the first laterals on the main stem, the plant will have a more finished appearance.

The espalier and fan forms of trained fuchsias are single-plant structures developed against a framework in the intial stages of growth but which, with careful and patient culture, will gradually envelop all structural supports as the plant matures to give a balanced

**Espaliers and Fans**

and symmetrical version of the chosen design.

Although, when judged on the show bench, these forms are viewed for frontal effect only, aspiring exhibitors should not be misled into thinking that no attention is paid to the rear of the plant. This should also be clothed with a good amount of clean, fresh foliage obscuring all sight of the supporting structure.

It is essential when growing this type of design that the correct growth habit is kept in mind when selecting the cultivar for this work. This should be vigorous, free branching and, most important, free flowering.

With both the fan and espalier designs a short stem or trunk must be shown to indicate a single plant structure and this must be allowed for when the rooted cutting is ready to be potted-up. If the fan shape is to be grown, the young cutting should be allowed to develop four pairs of leaves and then be stopped. This will initiate side growths below, from which are selected two pairs of laterals growing in the same direction. These will probably be the second and fourth pairs of laterals due to the cruciform shape of growth; the first and third pairs will be growing in the opposite direction and must be removed. Removal of the first pair will give the required short stem, the third pair being superfluous to the shape requirement. The established laterals are now stopped at one pair of leaves and if the chosen cultivar is short jointed a further stop may well be necessary at one pair of leaves, to encourage as many lateral growths as possible low down on the plant before growth extension of laterals becomes too pronounced.

A framework of the design must be supplied at an early stage of growth. Growths are tied to this while still soft and supple. This should not be delayed because, when two stops are made on each of the original four laterals there will be 16 growths all wanting to go in different directions. These must therefore be tied flat against the structure when small, if twisting of the stem is to be avoided with the consequent restriction in sap flow.

As growth proceeds, the leading shoots will be stopped from time to time to encourage further lateral growth required to fill out the ever expanding top section of the design. Once the envisaged height and width has been reached, attention must be given to stopping all side growths emanating from the basic framework of the plant to encourage further lateral growths that are so essential to build up a solid mass of leafy structure as a background for the flowers to come. This continual stopping of side growths has a twofold purpose: as well as building up a dense mass of foliage it also increases the number of flowering tips which, when stopping has ceased, should be tied in, in strategic positions spread evenly over the whole area of the design to ensure, as far as possible, an even

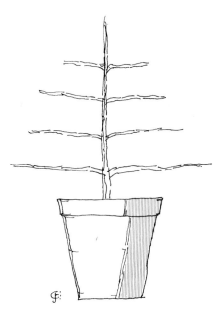

Figure 5.2
Basic Framework of
Young Plant
Intended for
Espalier Form

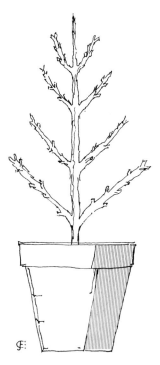

Figure 5.3
Basic Framework
of Young Plant
Trained for a
Fan Form

distribution of flower later on. It will be found that tying in flowering tips is necessary, because as the plant is presented as a flat structure, any uneven flower distribution will attract unfavourable attention on the show bench.

The general culture during the growing season will be the same as for all other specimen plants with attention to watering, feeding and the occasional mulch to the soil surface, using the usual potting compost. Mulching has an added benefit apart from the obvious addition of fresh soil. During hot weather, continual watering tends to wash away the soil surface leaving the top feeding roots exposed and if left in this state over a period of time they will eventually die off, and no plant with a multiplicity of side growth can afford to lose any of its feeding root system if cultural quality is to be maintained.

The espalier design is also originated from a short stem, but in this instance lateral growths are trained symmetrically in a horizontal position either side of a central stem which is trained in an upright position for the total height of the plant. A support suitable for the design shape must be supplied and lateral extension should be tied in as necessary to maintain a neat shape. Again the cruciform style of growth will probably necessitate removal of alternate laterals, and these should be rubbed out when small to avoid any lasting disfigurement to the main stem. If removal of laterals is the system preferred some thought should be given to the cultivar used as the length of stem between retained laterals will be doubled.

Espaliers and fans, as with the other more difficult cultural forms, may be grown on in succeeding years to achieve grand proportions. After the winter rest period, they are pruned, or more correctly 'spurred back', and generally thinned out, repotted into a pot at least one size smaller — this is easily done by teasing out as much of the old compost as possible — and once again starting into growth. Overhead spraying with clear water is beneficial and when new growth is observed the whole plant can be layed down to restrict sap flow and encourage strong lower lateral growth.

With a second-year plant one does of course have the added advantage of experience of the characteristics of the cultivar used.

Pillars

As a show plant, the pillar is rarely ever seen. There are several reasons for this, not least being the high cost of heating to keep them ticking over during the winter months, particularly in their first season of building up the main structure, when the leader is kept growing through the winter months to attain the height required in the shortest possible time. Transportation costs for large plants such as this are also high and, since space in the average

80

amateur's greenhouse is usually at a premium, this combination has no doubt contributed greatly to the decline in the popularity of the pillar together with that of the conical and pyramid forms.

At the turn of the century these forms were widely grown by gardeners on large estates when magnificent specimens were produced, often taking four years of almost daily attention to reach their peak. Specimens such as these, alas, will probably never be seen again, at least in any quantity.

However, the recently revised Judging Standard of the BFS does include a section dealing with requirements of cultural excellence for the pillar of both single and multiple plant structures, as indeed it does also for the conical and pyramid forms and it is interesting to note that there is no restriction on size. It would seem that the Society have left the door ajar to encourage growers to exhibit these forms once again, albeit on a much more reduced scale than may have previously been acceptable. The thought that we may yet see a return to popularity of these forms is quite exhilarating.

## The Single-Plant Structure

In outline, the pillar should appear as a tall graceful column with a constancy of diameter from top to bottom and, for show purposes, a short stem free of all growth is required to indicate a single-plant construction with the pot or container in good proportion to the plant.

A vigorous, free branching, medium-jointed cultivar is required and one's personal choice that includes these assets should be suitable. This can be rooted in the normal way and when ready is potted-up into the pot size that will comfortably accommodate the root system, but must not be over-potted. A cane support must be provided in this early stage to help prevent any deviation from upright growth and ties are attended to when required. Soft wire rings are excellent for this purpose, being easily fitted or removed when necessary.

To obtain good, fast growth with no checks, it is necessary to pot-on as quickly as possible. Therefore inspection of the root system should be done frequently. With pot sizes of up to 4 in inspection after about ten days from the previous potting will be necessary, and as soon as roots appear through the side of the root ball the plant must be potted-on to the next size pot. These very quick potting successions are essential to healthy, vigorous growth and must never be overlooked. At no time, when building the structure of any growth form, should roots be allowed to acquire the 'pot habit' as this can lead to a premature hardening of the stem and premature flowering. If root crowding is allowed to develop in the pot it can initiate flower buds in the leaf axils. Should this

81

occur when running up the stem for a pillar it will result in a loss of the lateral growth, thereby upsetting the balance of the plant. Once buds are initiated in the leaf axils it is usual for successive axils to follow suit, with the whole top section becoming a flowering tip. This will ruin the main stem if the total height has not been reached, as the only effective cure is to pinch out the offending section, back to a point where side shoots are emerging.

Under normal circumstances, with correct potting procedures and adequate watering, premature flowering will not arise and the main stem will grow without interruption.

The cane support should be changed as often as is required to keep several inches showing above the plant and should always be replaced in the hole from which the previous cane was taken to mini-mise possible damage to the root system. When the total height is reached the cane should be trimmed back to just below the foliage.

As growth proceeds, attention to laterals will become necessary. These should not be touched until such time as the plant has reached a pot size of approximately 9 in unless they have grown excessively long when the tips can be taken away to prevent them becoming unwieldy.

At the 9 in pot stage if all has gone well, the plant will be in the region of 3-3½ ft high and stopping of laterals can commence. A good tip when making the first stop on a pillar is to use the top diameter of the pot as a guide. If one looks down on the plant, directly over the cane support the top of the pot will be seen clearly and side growth may be pinched out to coincide with the rim of the pot. This will ensure that the diameter is constant from the start. Should a height of 6 ft be the ultimate aim it is recommended that a diameter of 18 in will give the finished plant a balanced appear-ance. It will not always be possible to maintain these exact dimen-sions, but they are a reasonable guide. Plants grown to any other sizes should be kept in the proportions of 1 in of diameter to every 4 in of height.

Subsequent stopping of laterals has a twofold purpose, both thickening the growth and giving body to the plant, as well as increasing the flowering mass.

Growing a pillar on a single stem can have certain disadvantages. It may for instance be found that lower lateral growths do not develop quite as well as one would like. The usual reason for this in young, fast-growing plants, is that the surge of energy is directed to the apex, and with the main stem in a vertical plane there is little or no restriction to the sap flow which can be to the detriment of basal growth. Should this arise, the rush of sap may be slowed down by the simple expedient of laying the plant down on its side in a horizontal position, although if this is resorted to, care must be taken to prevent damage to lateral growths. It must be remembered that while the plant is in the prostrate position, it should still be turned each day to equalise any effect of phototropism. If the grower intends to produce these rather large structures it may well be worthwhile to construct a device to support the pot and plant to facilitate the turning process, a difficulty that has in all probability deterred many enthusiasts from attempting this form of culture in the past. However, such a device need not be an insurmountable problem for the handyman and a little thought might suggest an arrangement of wooden blocks, in which to cradle the pot, from which a rod extends of a length similar to the height of the plant and at the end of which there might be a support similar to that of a fisherman's rod-rest, and of a height to maintain the main stem in the horizontal position. The sophistication of such a device may be left to the ingenuity of the individual.

If an odd lateral growth appears to be growing rather more slowly than its neighbours it can be induced to catch them up by tying it for a time in a more vertical position thereby increasing the sap flow, and conversely a lateral that is growing too fast can be made to slow down by the use of a weighted string to hold the lateral down thereby decreasing the sap flow. Weight strings are perhaps the most useful of training aids, and can quite easily be made from short lengths of twine or very thin string, to which are added rings of lead that can be cut from old lead piping, or by the addition of split lead-shot, increasing the weights as and when required.

When overwintering first season pillars or similar large specimen plants, it is necessary to keep them just ticking over. A temperature of 47°F should be sufficient to do this without the risk of unnecessary forced growth before the next growing season proper, when the ultimate shape is procured.

## Pruning Established Large-Specimen Plants

A period of dormancy is normal and beneficial to most plants that have matured and flowered in the previous season, but large plants such as these can present some problems when reactivating growth in the new season. It is therefore recommended that when restarting established plants into growth, the plant should be laid down to increase availability of sap to the lower regions and clear water should be sprayed over them once a day to help soften the older, harder wood.

As side growths are produced the opportunity to prune back to propitious growths should be taken before sap flow becomes too great, as excessive bleeding may result. However, severe pruning back into old wood before evidence of new growth is seen is extremely risky and may result in loss of growth entirely.

When satisfied that active basal growth is established the plant can be returned to the upright position and all later development will be directed to maintaining the desired shape.

### Twin Stemmed, Single-Plant Structures

Once again, a vigorous self-branching cultivar is selected and rooted in the normal way. The cutting is stopped at two or three pairs of leaves and the two lateral growths emanating from just below the stop are trained upright on cane supports. All other laterals and leaves below this are removed and will allow a single stem to be seen originating from soil level.

Figure 5.4
Initial Training of
a Twin-stemmed
Single Plant, Pillar

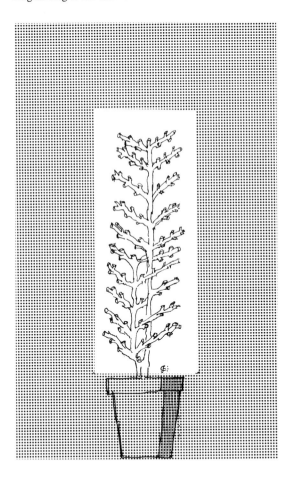

The object now is to grow one stem as a bush and the other as a standard. When it has been decided what total height is required, the weaker of the two upright growths must be pinched out at half the total height (see Figure 5.4). This is now treated as a bush and can have all the side laterals stopped at two pairs of leaves, the idea being that a much denser basal growth results than is possible with the single stemmed system. The second stem is grown on until it reaches the total height when the growing tip is removed. It is often advocated that at this point all lateral growth on the lower half of the standard stem be removed. If this is done regardless of the development to lateral growth on the bush side, it may be found that growth is removed that could have been used to make up deficiencies on the other stem. Therefore, it is advisable when removing lower growth on the standard stem, that only that which is surplus to requirements is taken away.

The stopping of laterals continues until such time as is necessary to allow development of flower buds. Eight weeks for single and ten weeks for double flowers from the last stop should see the peak of flowering perfection.

This type of structure is not constructed in one season, although it is possible with some very fast-growing cultivars to produce a fair height. These however will be found to lack generally the density of the second-year plant, if for no other reason than that much energy is directed to obtaining height in the initial stages of growth. For this reason the grower will have to decide whether or not to allow development of flowers in the first season, or dispense with flowers and direct all the plant's energy to vegetative growth, with an ultimate aim of greater stature in the second season.

*Multiple-Plant Structures*

For show purposes, the BFS now accepts pillars, conicals and pyramids of multiple-plant development and allows three plants of the same cultivar to be used in their constitution. Pillars grown on this system are expected to be of somewhat larger dimensions than those developed on one of the single-plant systems. These need not necessarily be of extreme height or diameter, but certainly of denser foliage and consequently more flower.

It may seem that the twin-stemmed pillar cultural method becomes unworkable with three plants and, for that reason one must adopt the pyramid or conical method of construction, i.e. stopping of main stems and running on a new leader.

Again, as with the other systems, potting-on, watering, renewal of supports, stopping, tying-up or lowering of laterals, and turning plants regularly to equalise the effects of phototropism must be constantly attended to if the potential of these specimen plants is to be achieved.

In all multiple-plant structures, main stems must be closely adjacent and tied neatly to stakes of good substance. If they are to be stood outside during the season of active growth, make sure that plants are well anchored down in the event of light summer breezes.

Pyramids

The pyramid form is probably the most difficult of all the shapes to train and is usually only attempted by the grower with more than average skill, much patience, and ample facilities to sustain growth over two seasons. It is no longer expected that plants of great proportions will be developed to equal those grown by the two masters of pyramid and pillar culture, Mr James Lye and Mr G. Bright. Space and devoted care, essential ingredients of pyramid culture, are rarely available in this modern age, and the skilled grower who wishes to test his or her ability will no doubt be well satisfied in producing plants some 6 ft in height with a base diameter of 4 ft.

A sturdy, vigorous cutting with a known potential for strong stiff lateral growths, freely produced, should be chosen and propagated in early spring. A fast, lush growth must be maintained throughout the building up process and at no time should a check in growth be tolerated. Careful and dedicated attention to potting successions is required together with routine feeding. The supplementary fertilisers must contain a predominance of nitrogen in the analysis to help maintain a soft vegetative growth for as long as possible through the first season.

Cuttings are rooted in the normal way and are grown on one stem to a height of approximately 9 in at which point the top is taken out (see Figure 5.5A). From this point two growths will result and are allowed to develop sufficiently to determine that one is growing with more vigour than the other. The weaker is then removed and the remaining growth is trained as the new leader (see Figure 5.5B). The developing lateral growths below this first stop will receive a temporary boost of energy due to the semi-restriction of the sap flow and this must be used to full advantage to extend the growth of the lower laterals, even resorting to laying the whole plant down if necessary. Attention to the development of the lower laterals cannot be overstressed. They must be given every opportunity to grow vigorously, for if left to their own devices they often give up in the race with the main stem. When the laterals below the first stop have developed sufficiently they must in turn be stopped and attention be given to the new leading growth which should be allowed to attain a height which allows the development of an equal number of laterals to that below the first stop, when the main stem is once again stopped to produce two new growths.

Again laterals must be encouraged below the stop and attention to feeding must not be overlooked. These laterals in turn are stopped and once again selection of a new main stem must be attended to. On this occasion, instead of selecting the stronger growth of the two, the one chosen is that which is opposite to the first stop on the main stem, the other one being removed (see Figure 5.6). At this juncture the basic training programme has been established and this procedure is continued until such time as the final height is reached. This will be a personal choice and is only dictated by the base diameter which must be kept in proportion to the height to balance the whole structure.

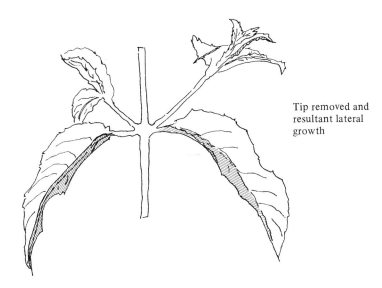

Figures 5.5A and B
Initial Stopping
Procedure in
Pyramid Training

Tip removed and
resultant lateral
growth

Weaker growth
subsequently removed
leaving new leader
to be trained on

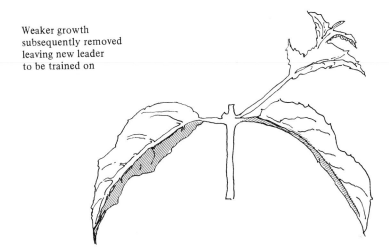

Figure 5.6
Further Stages of
Pyramid Training

The alternate stopping of the main stem and the lateral growth below it, is designed to restrict the flow of sap in the main stem sufficiently to stimulate the growth below. This is very important and it should never be taken for granted that lateral growth will develop smoothly and in accordance with that of the main stem. It is very rare to find any cultivar that will do this of its own accord and every effort must be made to ensure maximum growth extension on laterals, particularly on those at the base of the plant, which are often developing during that time of the season when light levels are low and growth is concentrated on main stem extension.

The pyramid is another of the larger structures that takes at least two seasons to develop into a specimen plant, and because of this the winter period at the end of the first season will see the plant in continued growth for which a temperature of not less than 47°F must be maintained. Over-watering should be avoided during this period and the use of fertiliser should be withheld, although it is beneficial to give a top dressing to the pot soil. It is usual when building up a plant of this type to remove all flowers and buds during the first flowering season enabling all energy to be directed to building up the structure. If this is the chosen method the spring of the second year will be planned to produce the ultimate shape and the known growth habit must be used to control the overall shape and flower production. The final pot size may well be around 14 in, and the heavier the better.

Subsequent treatment for mature plants involves pruning the whole plant back, while maintaining the shape, and removing as much of the old soil as possible in order to re-pot down in size. As with the pillar, when encouraging new growth in the spring, the plant can be laid down as near horizontal as possible to slow down the sap flow, and when basal growth has been initiated the plant is returned to the upright.

The conical is the last of the three really large structures in which the fuchsia can be grown. This elegant show piece is unlike the pyramid in that the lower circumference is reduced in size and the whole plant tapers finely to the apex, the height attained being related to the diameter as in that of a tall elegant tree. The cultural method is similar to that of a pillar, the only real difference being the taper effect.

**Conicals**

To create this, a free-branching cutting is selected and after rooting is allowed to grow on a single stem with a cane support. Although show schedules do not lay down specific dimensions, a plant with a height of 6 ft and a base diameter of 3 ft will produce a correct shape, providing attention is given to the taper. This will be achieved by judicial stopping throughout the growing season. Again the plant must be maintained at a minimum temperature of $47°F$ through the winter months to keep the top slowly growing. A light pruning to the lower section will probably be required in the spring, to maintain the correct taper.

This is a recent innovation for the show bench, and is basically designed to enable growers with a limited area of glass to grow all of the plant forms previously described, but in miniature. These Lilliputian plants are not products of restricted root growth (i.e. Bonsai), but scaled down versions of the usual plant forms. They create exciting possibilities from the point of view of exhibiting as well as for the enthusiast who would like to try his or her skill at

**Small Pot Culture**

something a little more testing than the run-of-the-mill shrub and bush forms.

It will be appreciated that the choice of cultivar will need critical assessment if one's aim is to produce plants of show quality. However, there are many of the smaller-flowered, slower-growing types that are eminently suitable, including some of the species from the Encliandra section Breviflorae.

Pyramids, conicals, pillars, espaliers, fans and standards will be constructed on similar lines as previously described, but strict control over growth must be maintained at all times to ensure conformity to the plant form definition. An example of this would be the difference in taper between a conical and a pyramid, which would not be so obviously pronounced in the smaller form.

Standards will have a maximum stem length of 10 in from soil level to the first branch, and the maximum diameter of a basket will be 6 in. Baskets of this size are not available commercially, but can be made from chicken wire. Size limits have been formulated for show purposes: a total height of 20 in and a maximum pot diameter of 5 in.

Exhibiting

There can be little doubt that much of the popularity enjoyed by the fuchsia today, has been stimulated to a large extent by the many exhibitions and competitions staged annually throughout the country. Many people receive their introduction to the fuchsia either from a friend or neighbour who has already been ensnared by the world of show fuchsias, or from visiting a flower show.

With a season that begins in May, at the Chelsea Flower Show, when the specialist fuchsia nurserymen stage their trade exhibits, through mid-season and the BFS's competitions at Sale, Birmingham, Reading and at the Royal Horticultural Hall, Westminster, to the Southport Flower Show and the last of the local societies shows in September, it is perhaps inevitable that this interloper to our shores has endeared itself to our hearts.

It is very difficult to find any other pot-grown plant that will give such a varied wealth of colour displayed over such a long period, and this, coupled to its amenability to training to almost any shape that can be devised, makes the fuchsia so adaptable to the show bench.

To produce plants of show quality should perhaps be the aim of all growers. Even if the intention is not to exhibit them, much pleasure and satisfaction will be experienced in attempting to produce the perfect plant and, if this standard of culture is achieved, the novice grower may find it hard to resist the temptation to test his or her skill on the show bench.

To anyone embarking on the very pleasant pastime of growing fuchsias for the show bench, possibly the best advice that can be given is that they should not expect instant success, and two years' growing experience with some cultivars that are to form the basis of their collection is necessary for most beginners before they can really hope to make an impression at any of the big shows. However, during this time much knowledge will be acquired, which can be augmented by joining one of the many local fuchsia societies that flourish throughout the country. These are, without doubt, an ideal stepping-stone for the beginner who wishes to test his or her skill against the more experienced growers and showmen, most of whom are usually only too willing to help the interested novice.

Familiarity with the BFS's *Handbook of Plant Form Definition and Judging Criteria* is a prerequisite of all exhibitors who seek guidance on cultural requirements and standards of perfection, and equally important is a complete understanding of the Show Schedule.

Although most local specialist societies adopt the BFS wording for the majority of their classes, the odd or unusual class is sometimes added to fill a local need, which, unless carefully worded, can have a different meaning read into it. In such instances, the judge will seek clarification from the Show Secretary, abiding by his ruling, so that an exhibitor who does not bother to seek help from the same source may be unfortunate enough to find that his class card has been marked NAS (not as schedule).

Fortunately such occurrences are rare, but it illustrates the care that is necessary and the need to consult the show officials on any class wording that may appear to be ambiguous in requirement. It may also save bitter disappointment and possible bad feeling against the judge, unless the reason is understood by the exhibitor before he leaves the show. The standard of competition at the shows of the local societies is quite high, as is also the standard of judging. However, it should be expected and accepted by exhibitors intending to compete in the competitions organised and drawn up by the BFS that they be strongly contested, attracting, as they do, many of the country's best growers.

Here the beginner and novice exhibitor will find that a much more strict standard of judging will prevail, and rightly so, because these are the shows that set the standard that every showman wishes to achieve.

Many disappointments experienced on the show bench can be attributed to careless inattention to simple cultural requirements. One of the saddest reasons for downgrading an otherwise good plant is the growers failure to observe and rectify the affects of phototropism on the plant during its early formative culture. Effectual remedy is rarely satisfactory in the latter stages of growth, despite intricate attempts forcibly to re-establish symmetry of growing shape or form with stakes and ties just prior to staging.

Should it be thought that the use of stakes is frowned upon by judges, it should be clearly understood that the judicious use of these aids to dress a plant for show purposes might well be used to better effect, to lift and fill gaps occasioned by sheer weight of bloom on the odd branch or two. Staging exhibits to their best possible advantage is expected and very desirable, particularly when staging multi-pot entries.

A well balanced and attractively staged exhibit, combined with general attention to overall cleanliness of presentation, can and does influence the final decision in close competition, when all other cultural requirements have been assessed as equally meritorious with its nearest rival.

All exhibitors are naturally desirous of presenting an entry that has an ascendancy of bloom over its rivals, but over-enthusiasm in this respect can lead to the temptation of leaving declining blooms on the plant, or the greater sin of physically opening immature flower buds. Both are unjustifiable and injurious to reputations.

Another pitfall that might well entrap the unwary novice is the need to dress their plants after staging. So many newcomers just put their plants on the table and walk off leaving the poor plant looking just as it was when it was taken out of the van that had transported it to the show. However much trouble and care is taken to minimise any possible damage to the plants during the journey, one thing is certain, and that is that much of the bloom will be shaken down into the growth of the plant. The obvious remedy must be applied: all blooms should be lifted up to the surface and arranged for the best effect (this can be particularly advantageous if the plant has been grown in the dense compact style when flowers can be arranged almost at will over the surface of the plant and used to good effect to cover any odd spots that would otherwise appear bare). This arrangement of blooms when exhibiting show plants is in no way classed as fraudulent; it is merely making the most of what there is, always providing that the bloom is still attached to the plant and has not just been laid there for the purpose of deception.

All good judges take a look underneath the foliage during their examination of a plant, so before you walk off, leaving the plant to its fate, make sure that there are no cobwebs, dead or yellowing leaves, pests or dead blooms to be seen. Older plants that have any signs of loose bark fibres should be gone over and cleaned.

The classification of a single flowered cultivar is that of one displaying four petals on each flower. Any flower that has five, six or seven petals is classified as semi-double, and flowers with more than seven petals are classed as full doubles.

For some years now there have been certain abnormalities appearing in various cultivars, and many plants that have been classified as single in the past have been showing a quantity of flowers with either five sepals or five petals. Therefore exhibitors intending to exhibit plants in classes for single-flowered plants should make sure that their entries do not display flowers of this type.

If it is found that plants are displaying a few flowers of this type, they should be removed. However, if the position is reversed and the plant should display a greater quantity of five-petaled flowers, it may still be possible to use the plant for exhibition by removing the true single flowers, providing that this does not leave the plant short of bloom, and exhibiting it as a semi-double, which at most shows are included in full double classes. It is possible that the occasion will arise when a plant will display half of its blooms as true singles and the rest with five petals and removal of either would deplete the flowering mass to such an extent that it would be useless for exhibition purposes. In a case such as this there is only one thing to do: enjoy it at home, but keep it away from the show bench and certain disappointment with a card marked NAS. Another point that should also be checked is the number of sepals displayed; any flower that has five or more is abnormal; all flowers, single or double, should only have four.

A plant that is used for exhibition should be in perfect condition. It should be symmetrical in shape, the leaves clean and free of pests and in a turgid condition, the flowers fresh and fully open and the container clean. The addition of a clean label legibly written, together with a mulch of fresh compost to the soil surface, can only enhance the appearance of the exhibit.

Stakes and ties should be as inconspicuous as possible. The former should be trimmed so that they do not protrude above the foliage, and the quantity used should also be kept to a minimum, because although the foliage will hide much of the staking system, any loss of foliage near the bottom of the plant will reveal more stakes than stems, and no accredited judge will ever consider the sight of these as 'cultural excellence'. Ties should be trimmed so that they are as small as possible; an inch of yellow bast, after each knot is made, will never enhance the neatness of any plant; soft wire rings, or a thin, green tying material will be much less conspicuous.

The sheer weight of flower on a branch will often be the cause of loss of symmetrical shape and, if disregarded, possible loss of the branch. Support should therefore be given so that the branch is returned to the most favourable position.

Another point that is often overlooked by the beginner, is the pot in which his exhibit is being shown. The schedule may state: One Plant, Single, any variety, in pot not exceeding 6 in in diameter, which seems straightforward enough, but, in this sense 'pot' means standard pot, that is, one with its vertical height the same as the diameter; so don't be caught out by using a dwarf pot (or half pot as they are sometimes termed), the depth of which is less than the diameter.

Transportation of plants to shows is also something that the beginner should give some thought to. The seasoned exhibitor has devised many ingenious ways of protecting plants during transportation to shows, but perhaps the two most important considerations are to reduce the movement of the growth above the pot and the movement of the plant and the pot within the transporting vehicle. The latter can be achieved by making a pot stand, quite simply, from a block of wood about 5 in square by ¾ in thick and driving three or four 6 in nails into it at an angle to correspond with that of the pot side and at equidistant intervals around the periphery of a previously inscribed circle, the diameter of which should match that of the base of the pot being used.

When making up this type of stand it may be prudent first to drill holes in which to insert the nails to prevent splitting the wood. It will be found that this type of stand will afford much more stability to an often top-heavy plant and is well worth the effort involved. The movement of the plant growth can also be effectively eliminated by the use of stockinette, which is a tubular material sold by most good builders merchants, also referred to as builders roll or scrim. A length of this material should be cut off the roll, approximately 2 ft in length and, with some assistance, the whole plant, pot first, should be enclosed within, by gradually drawing the scrim up and round the plant to the top where it will be found that it will close over the top of the plant, effectively encasing the whole in a protective cocoon. Removal should be effected from the bottom first, gradually rolling and easing the material up to the top where it can be easily removed. This may seem to be a rather dubious and elaborate method of protection, but is that which is used most frequently and effectively by growers today.

Growing and exhibiting fuchsias should be fun, and this is the spirit in which it should be undertaken. If a decision should go against you on the show bench, accept it with good grace — remember the judge is not there to denigrate your plants, he will not know who they belong to, and is assessing a group of plants against a set of cultural standards of perfection, analytically, not with any sense of bias. Most judges welcome enquiries from exhibitors after the completion of their duties, and are only too pleased to be able to qualify their decisions. After all, he is the only one who can give

Citation

Gruss Aus dem Bodethal

Hula Girl

Royal Velvet

Tristesse

Swanley Gem

Blush of Dawn

Mrs Marshall

Pink Lady

Hobsons Choice

Lena Dalton

Leanora

Westminster Chimes

Countess of Aberdeen

Bobby Shafto

Lady Kathleen Spence

you an answer; no show secretary, organiser, steward, officer of the society or even another judge can be expected to give you a correct reason for a particular decision by any judge.

## BFS Judging Procedure

It is not expected that an experienced judge should be required to use score cards on his/her rounds of judging.

The experienced judge acquires the ability of balancing all the factors entering his/her decisions into a just and unbiased evaluation, based on all the various principles and facts fixed in the criteria.

The BFS strongly recommend that no judge, however experienced, should be asked or required to judge any class on his/her own.

It is usual that the judges look over the entire section or class involved to determine the overall average quality of the group, which will also give a guide to the overall rating of the exhibits.

This done, the manifestly inferior entries will be eliminated for lack of cultural competence or non-conformity to the schedule, etc., and the remaining entries are then subjected to a more detailed scrutiny, and evaluation will continue until the final decision is made.

Plants marked NAS (not as schedule) will not be elegible for a prize, cup or trophy or other type of award at that show. All judges must be fully conversant with the show schedule. Judges may remove plants for closer inspection and every endeavour to replace as found will be taken.

## Judging Criteria

Cultural excellence and quality of growth is of prime importance, consideration will always be given to the difficulty of culture in different plants.

Prematurely opened buds, defoliated expanses of lateral growths and discoloured or damaged leaves, detract from perfection and will be penalised accordingly.

Flowers will be appraised on their state of perfection, whether the majority are in fresh full bloom in bud state, or past their peak.

Flowers must be typical in size, colour and form for the particular fuchsia. Quality and distribution of flowers must be appropriate to the cultivar or species concerned. General grooming and presentation are important factors in close and difficult decisions.

Containers must be clean. Soil surfaces must be free of moss, weed, dead flowers and leaves or other debris. Plants must be in good proportion to container size.

Plants must be growing on own roots. Stakes and ties if used must

British Fuchsia Society's Handbook of Plant Form Definition and Judging Criteria

95

be inconspicuous and neat.

Plants must be free of pest and disease; unsightly insecticide powders or residues must be removed.

## Ethics

It is acknowledged that personal preferences and prejudices are held by some judges. It is therefore important to recognise this fact and to be particularly careful not to be swayed by essentially personal views.

Having been selected as an accredited judge by qualification of knowledge and experience of fuchsias and a clear understanding of the standard of judging recommended by the BFS, it is expected that the duties as a judge will be performed in a manner courteous and dignified at all times.

## Stewards

It is of course, the judges' responsibility to see that exhibits are according to schedule; but it is here that efficient stewardship can be of immense value to the judges by ensuring that all exhibits conform to the requirements of the class. For example, individual entries must not have too few or too many specimens in multiple-pot classes.

Stewards should make sure that all entry cards face downwards and should be ready to check pot sizes and lengths of stem if confirmation is required.

The stewards should clearly indicate the start and finish of each class and the total number of entrants. As soon as the class has been judged all cards should be turned faced upwards and appropriate awards cards affixed to commended exhibits.

Two stewards would be the ideal number, so that the whole process can be carried out in the very limited time before the public are admitted.

Stewards should not engage judges in distracting conversation during the period of judging. The judges would be only too pleased to answer questions after completion of their task.

The role of a steward is one of privilege and esteem: he is the confidant of the judges who, in turn, would expect their trust honoured.

## Shrub

A shrub fuchsia is a plant that has the quality of being shrubby, i.e. producing shoots from below soil level in addition to the main trunk and its lateral growths.

These types should be grown freely but with a little judicious training to obtain a balanced plant. An abundance of foliage and flower over entire plant, according to variety, viewed from all sides and top. Plant in good proportion to container size.

*Cultural Proficiency.* An abundance of vigorous growth, receiving but little formal training to acquire a balanced plant, overall quality, freshness and full coverage of foliage and flower, according to variety, to be maintained over entire plant top to bottom.

No special shape or form is required, other than good balance being achieved when viewed from all sides.

### Bush

A bush plant is developed on a short stem free of all growth for a max. of 1½ in to indicate clearly a single plant. The entire plant should be covered with an abundance of foliage and flower according to variety, presenting a balanced symmetrical plant viewed from all angles. Plant in good proportion to container size.

*Cultural Proficiency.* Overall quality of plant growth, uniformity and fullness of growth when viewed from all sides. Foliage should be abundant and clean, over entire body of plant. Stakes, if used should be limited.

### Basket (Full)

This type of growth is one in which an optional number of plants are grown in a wire or plastic basket to be viewed from top and sides when displayed in an elevated position.

Plant growth must fill centre and top of basket and continue to surge over edge in a sweeping cascade. Uniform growth, clean leaf and an abundance of flower, according to variety, must continue to at least the depth of the container and should be evenly distributed from crown to end of trailing growths. The container should not be visible when viewed from eye level. Size of basket not to exceed that stated in schedule.

*Cultural Proficiency.* Number of plants optional, growth should cover centre and top of basket and surge over the edge in a sweeping cascade of evenly distributed hanging branches. An abundance of foliage and flower hanging to a depth of at least the depth of the basket is required. Quality and general excellence of culture.

### Basket (Wall or Half Basket)

This type of growth is similar in many ways to a full basket except that it is designed to hang on, or be attached to, a wall and, is viewed from the top, front and sides.

The number of plants is optional and should cover entire crown and surge over front and sides of container to present a fully balanced evenly distributed display of abundant leaf and flower, according to variety, covering crown to end of trailing branches. The container should not be visible. Size of basket should not exceed that stated in schedule.

*Cultural Proficiency.* Number of plants optional, growth must be of good balance, good crown coverage draping to edges and continuing over in a cascade effect. An abundance of leaf and flower, according to variety, over entire head and trailing branches to a depth at least to that of container to present a fully balanced, evenly distributed display, viewed from top, front and sides. Container should not be visible.

### Standards (Full)

Height of stem clear of all growth shall be from soil level to first lateral not less than 30 in and not exceeding 42 in. The trunk shall be straight, free of knots or other ugly blemishes and may be supported by a stake. The total head should be a profusion of branches, presenting a full and balanced effect of lush foliage and flower, according to variety, over entire head. Plant should be in proportion to container size.

*Cultural Proficiency.* Overall quality of plant growth. Uniformity and fullness of growth when viewed from all sides, well furnished with clean foliage and flower, according to variety. Plant to present a well balanced effect. The stem should be straight and true, free of all blemishes caused by removal of laterals.

### Standards (Half)

Height of stem clear of all growth from soil level to first branch to be not less than 18 in nor exceed 30 in. Cultural details as for full standards.

### Standard (Quarter or Table)

Height of stem clear of all growth from soil level to first branch to be not less than 12 in nor exceeding 18 in. Head of good overall balance. Cultural details, etc., as for full standard.

### Ball

As its growth type suggests, a near ball shape is required. One or more plants should be trained into a globular shape around the container and, when fully developed, the pot is obscured.

An abundance of good leaf and flower, according to variety, over entire growth. Branching system should not be evident when viewed from any angle. No stakes are allowed. Spacers, if used, should be removed.

*Cultural Proficiency*. Skill of the grower in correctly developing the plant to a specific growth type. Uniformity, balance and fullness of ball growth when viewed all sides and crown. Freshness and an abundance of clean foliage and flower, according to variety, should obscure the branching system and envelope the container. Plant in good proportion to container size.

## Espalier and Fans

Espaliers and fans are single plants trained on a latticed structure. The laterals should be matched symmetrically on both sides of the plant centre. Espaliers should have horizontally trained laterals, and fans should have laterals trained in a fan design.

Whether structural design originates from a central trunk, extending entire height of plant, or from a chosen number of basic laterals, a short trunk consistent with overall plant size or development will be shown, free of all growth, to indicate single plant structure. All laterals to be fully covered with foliage and flower, according to variety.

Plant to be in good proportion to container size viewed from front.

*Cultural Proficiency*. The basic factors for all types will be the skill of developing the chosen design into an arranged balance of symmetrically matched laterals on both sides of plant centre. Although viewed for frontal effect, the rear of the latticed structure should be well covered with good clean foliage. All laterals must be fully covered in good proportion and, general excellence of growth quality will be considered. Height of trunk to first lateral shall be minimum consistent with overall size or development of plant.

Plant should be of good proportion to container size.

## Pillar (Single-Plant Structure)

A single-plant growth developed to produce a uniformly cylindrical structure. Fully covered with foliage and flowers. A short section of stem from soil level to first laterals must be shown to clearly indicate single-plant structure.

The relation of height to diameter and constancy of diameter from bottom to top of plant should produce, when viewed from all sides, a graceful column or pillar of abundant foliage and flower, according to variety. Overall plant size is unrestricted. Plant to be of good proportion to container size.

*Cultural Proficiency*. Degree of skill shown in developing plant into a uniformly cylindrical structure. A short stem free of growth to indicate a single plant structure must be shown.

Diameter of pillar must be maintained from bottom to top of plant. The relation of height to diameter must be that of a tall graceful column, well covered with foliage and flowers, according to variety. The plant must be of good proportion to pot size, which is unrestricted.

### Pillar (Multiple-Plant Structure)

Three plants of the same variety go into this pillar. Main stems shall be closely adjacent and tied neatly to a central stake. It is expected that through the use of multiple plants the height and diameter will be larger than single-plant pillars. The relation of diameter to height must be maintained to present a tall graceful pillar of foliage and flower. Width or diameter shall remain constant from bottom to top. Plant should be in good proportion to container size.

*Cultural Proficiency.* Degree of skill in developing a taller and relatively fuller pillar than that of the single-plant structure.

The three stems must be closely adjacent and tied to a central stake. It will be expected to produce a great volume of foliage and consequently a greater production of flower, according to variety. The relation of height to diameter will be assessed and the ability to maintain a constant diameter or width over the entire plant, bottom to top.

### Pyramid (Single-Plant Structure)

A single-plant growth developed to produce a uniformly tapering structure from bottom to top. The pyramid shape shall be maintained when viewed from all sides. A short trunk to clearly indicate single-plant structure must be shown. The relation of height to diameter of lowest section should be that of a tall tapering tree fully covered with foliage and flower overall, according to container size. Central stake allowed.

*Cultural Proficiency.* Skill of development to achieve a uniformly tapering pyramid on a single-plant structure. A short stem free of growth must be shown to clearly indicate single-plant structure. The taper shall be uniform from bottom to top of plant and be constant when viewed from all sides. Height of plant in relation to lowest section shall be tall and tapering, fully covered with foliage and flowers, according to variety. Plant size is unrestricted but good balance is expected overall. Plant in good proportion to container size.

*Pyramid (Multiple-Plant Structure)*

Three or more plants of the same variety go into this pyramid. Main stems will be closely adjacent and tied neatly to a central stake. It is expected that through the use of multiple plants height and diameter will be greater than single-plant structure entries and consequently denser foliage and flower, according to variety. No restriction on size of plant. Good overall balance should be achieved. Plants in good proportion to container size. All other criteria compared on an equitable basis.

*Cultural Proficiency.* Skill of development to achieve uniformly tapering pyramid. The taper shall be uniform from bottom to top of plant and be constant when viewed from all sides. It is expected that through the use of multiple plants height and diameter will be greater than that of single-plant structure, foliage denser and flower production greater, according to variety. The multiple stems must be closely adjacent and tied neatly to central stake. Plant must be in good proportion to container size.

*Conical (Single-Plant Structure)*

A single-plant growth developed to produce a finely tapering structure. Dissimilar to pyramid in that the lower section is reduced in circumference and tapers gradually and finely to the apex. A short stem free of growth is shown to clearly indicate single-plant growth. The relation of height to diameter shall be tall and slender, gracefully tapering to a fine apex. Fully covered with good foliage and flower, according to variety. Plant size is unrestricted. Plant to be in good proportion to container size.

*Cultural Proficiency.* Degree of skill shown in developing a uniform structure into a true conical growth. From a single plant a gradual taper must be maintained from bottom to apex and must be constant around the circumference. Good foliage and flower in overall quantity to achieve a well balanced, slender and elegant plant. Plant in good proportion to container size.

*Conical (Multiple-Plant Structure)*

Three plants go into this conical. Main stems shall be in close proximity and tied to a central stake. It is expected that through the use of multiple plants height and diameter will be larger than single-plant structures and consequently a greater volume of flower and foliage, according to variety, expected. Good balance required. Size of plant is unrestricted. Plant to be in good proportion to container size.

101

*Cultural Proficiency.* Skill of developing a taller and relatively fuller plant than the single-plant structure. A greater volume of flower and foliage, according to variety, is expected and good balance must be achieved. Constancy of taper must be maintained from the lower section to a fine tapering apex. Plant in good proportion to container size.

### Small Pot Culture

A number of fuchsia cultivars and species are eminently suitable for this type of culture and are normally found among the smaller flowered types. Late rooting of cuttings is practised and these plants can be trained to any of the plant form definitions previously described in detail.

All growths and maximum pot sizes will be limited to the sizes listed below. Smaller growth examples to be proportionate to pot size.

True proportions of plant form will be expected. Good foliage and flowers, typical in size, form and colour for plant exhibited. Relative difficulty of plant form chosen will be recognised and given full consideration.

Pyramids, conicals, pillars, espaliers and fans will be allowed a maximum of 20 in in height (soil level to apex) with a maximum pot size of 5 in.

Standards will have a maximum of 10 in from soil level to first branch and a maximum pot size of 5 in.

Baskets will be a maximum of 6 in diameter.

### Affiliated Societies Display

The prime consideration of this entry will be attractiveness of arrangement, design, colour, harmonies and contrasts.

Quality of plants: fresh flower and clean healthy foliage in total overall display. Structural paraphernalia, pots, etc., should be restricted from view.

*Judging Criteria.* Skill of arrangement, attractive design and/or originality. Good use of colour harmony or contrast. Quality of plant material. Structural paraphernalia and pots restricted from view.

### Species

These should be grown freely, or with minimum amount of training that will promote branching. Decorative fruit may be allowed to develop as an added attraction.

Clean foliage and fresh flower, and/or fruit is expected. Stakes or other training media may be used.

*Cultural Proficiency.* A vigorous flourishing plant growth, with quantity of foliage, flowers and/or fruit appropriate to species concerned. Overall quality typical of species shown. Plant in good proportion to container size. All species should be correctly named. Soil surface clean, free of weeds, moss or other debris. Label neat, clean and legible.

## Species Type (Excluding Encliandra)

These should be grown freely, or with minimum amount of training that will promote branching. Decorative fruit may be allowed to develop as an added attraction.

Clean foliage and fresh flower, and/or fruit is expected. Stakes or other training media may be used.

*Cultural Proficiency.* A vigorous flourishing plant growth, with quantity of foliage, flowers and/or fruit appropriate to species concerned. Overall quality typical of species shown. Plant in proportion to container size. All plants should be correctly named. Soil surface clean, free of weed, moss or other debris. Label neat clean and legible.

## Encliandra Section (Breviflorae)

Species and hybrids may be exhibited in these classes, but they should be correctly named.

*Cultural Proficiency.* An abundance of healthy growth, overall freshness and high quality of foliage and flower. The decorative fruit may be left on the plant. Formal training should be minimal. No special shape or form is required other than a pleasing aesthetic effect. See Judging Criteria for detailed consideration for all features.

## Individual Blooms

Blooms must be clean, free of damage, disease or pest. Flower should be typical in form and colour of the cultivar or species and in full bloom state, complete with all floral parts including pedicel. All normal fuchsia flowers show four sepals; those displaying more will not be accepted in this class.

*Judging Criteria.* Blooms true to form. Prime condition. Fully open complete with all parts free of blemish, disease, pest, etc. Colour true to cultivar in full bloom. All floral parts, excepting the anthers, should be free of pollen. Correct identification of cultivar or species clearly visible on cards provided.

## Groom Your Plants

Water plants with systemic insecticide a week before the show, and again a day or two before entering the exhibition hall. Insecticide powder residues can be removed with a fine mist spray containing a small amount of Stergene. This will in no way harm the plant.

Look out for slugs on pots and plants, especially if grown outside.

Check plants thoroughly for signs of disease. *Do not* bring diseased plants to the hall under any circumstances.

Remove all debris from soil surface. A layer of fresh soil or wet peat will give your entry a neat, clean look and also help to retain moisture.

Check condition of container, if badly chipped or cracked, a fresh container is in order. Badly stained containers can be cleaned with chlorine bleach.

Check all supports and ties. Renew supports if required, and change location of ties if cutting into trunk or stem. Before you leave your entry, removed damaged or discoloured leaves, remove blooms that are past their best and remove seed pods, except, as in some classes for species, retention is specified.

*Dress your plant,* i.e. lift blooms to the fore if hidden under the foliage.

*Show day is the culmination of all your efforts, don't let yourself down by disregard to detail.*

# CHAPTER 6

# Fuchsias in the Greenhouse

The greenhouse owner enjoys, among a number of other advantages, an extended season of plant growth and an ability to garden in comfort no matter what the weather may be. These two factors alone are probably sufficient to urge the grower to invest in the purchase of a greenhouse and, if he so decides, his obvious first concern is the type of greenhouse best suited to the culture of pot plants. The best choice is of course the type with a brick wall to staging level — not only does it make a solid structure but also provides for a minimum heat loss, and will be appreciated in long-term running costs when providing artificial heating. Alternatively and much easier to erect are the wood boarded to staging level type, which are usually very well made and can give excellent results.

Having decided and purchased your greenhouse, siting must now be considered and if water and electricity are to be installed a site as near as possible to these amenities must be considered if installation costs are to be kept to a minimum. The site should provide full light and be well drained.

Electric heating, thermostatically controlled, has much to commend itself to the average amateur, and can be easily installed by a competent electrician. An electrically heated soil warmed propagating bench can be effectively used to reduce the overall heating cost of the greenhouse if manipulated as explained elsewhere.

Controlling the atmosphere in a greenhouse can at times be difficult to manage, but the first rule one must clearly understand is the need to ventilate at all times. Never close down completely even during the coldest and dampest spells in an effort to contain heat, for this creates a highly humid and stagnant atmosphere, a condition that holds great danger in the cultivation of young plants. Although the plants may appear to be growing well the truth is that they are too full of water and growth is too rapid and soft. Such plants if subjected to sudden changes of temperature or humidity, rapidly become victims to fungus disease leading eventually to total collapse and loss.

In the true sense, ventilation should be interpreted as air movement or circulation, and it will be appreciated that such movement cannot be achieved by opening the top vents only. Most modern greenhouse structures usually provide side vents at staging level on which the plants are growing, and while these are particularly useful during the summer months, they are not really practical during the winter and it therefore becomes essential to install vents which allow air to enter at a lower point. Plastic sliding shutters mounted over air-bricks in the lower parts of the wall are really all that is needed to provide sufficient movement of air.

As the days lengthen, sudden bursts of spring sunshine will need to be attended to and some form of shading will be required, because although these bursts are of short duration the rays through glass can be quite fierce and the possibility of leaf scorch on tender young plants must be avoided. Any type of muslin material is adequate as a temporary shade but management can be tiresome due to the frequency of removal and replacement. The most satisfactory answer to this problem would be blinds that can be easily let down or drawn up as required, and by far the best material for this purpose is the fine plastic netting of about 1/8 in mesh that allows dispersed sunlight to enter without harming young plants. With warmer days and longer spells of brilliant sunshine, full ventilation and the provision of some type of permanent shading on the glass might well be considered. There are a number of these on the market which are easily applied with a spray or a brush, some of which are electrostatic and are not washed off by rain but can be removed with a dry cloth.

Watering and the creation of a moist atmosphere should be attended to as early in the day as possible, spraying over and between the pots and directly on to the staging and greenhouse floor. This will provide the buoyant atmosphere so necessary to good culture. Overhead spraying should not be practised when plants are showing buds or flower, as this can mark the flowers, particularly if water collects in upturned sepals.

Cleanliness in the greenhouse is vital if one is to produce healthy plants; clear out any accumulated rubbish from under the staging and never leave dead or decaying plant material around. Make the house clean and keep it clean. Spray against all possible insect attacks regularly, alternating if possible with several different types of insecticides or an occasional smoke bomb, as this does help to prevent a build up of resistance or immunity to one particular type of control.

Be prepared to give your time to the culture of first-class plants and the effort will be repaid a hundredfold.

# CHAPTER 7

# Pests and Pest Control

The range of insecticides made available to the amateur grower is limited by government regulations which restrict availability of the more poisonous substances to commercial growers. But even so, many insecticides readily available to the amateur are extremely poisonous in concentration and every precaution should be taken to avoid indiscriminate usage and personal contact with the substance.

Makers' recommended dilution rates must always be strictly followed when making a spray solution. High concentrations are not necessarily more effective against pests and could in many cases cause severe damage to the plants. After each spraying programme, thoroughly rinse out the sprayer and wash your hands and any other areas of skin that may have been exposed to spray drift. Always keep insecticide bottles safely away from children and animals and make sure they keep away from treated plants.

Self-contained, low-pressure aerosol sprays are without doubt a boon to the amateur and although designed primarily for the greenhouse, can be used outside with good effect on a still day. These press-button aerosols discharge a very fine atomised spray of insecticide up and over the plants. Do not aim directly on to the foliage as the solvent used in aerosols may cause damage.

Amateurs have available to them several systemic chemicals usually applied by drenching the root soil, there to be transmitted throughout the plant sap. Others can be applied as a spray or aerosol, to be absorbed by the leaves into the sap. All do a good job. However, some are more effective against specific insects or mites than others and it is perhaps best that one should consult the literature or labels of different commercial offerings and purchase the one best suited to particular needs. All systemics are rather expensive and are normally only used for pot work under glass, being particularly effective against red spider.

**Systemic Insecticides**

107

Fumigation is a very effective means of destruction for various pests and mites, particularly if suffering from a heavy infestation.

Excellent results can be obtained against aphids, capsid bug, red spider mite, white fly, etc. Products containing gamma — HCH are excellent for control of all sucking pests.

Whilst fumigation is in progresss the door should be locked if possible, and it is advisable to display a notice indicating the hazard. Any holes or cracks in the greenhouse from which the fumigant may prematurely escape should be sealed beforehand, as a light breeze outside will quickly disperse the fumigant inside the green-house and may nullify your efforts. A useful tip when using this type of insect control is to make sure that there is a moist atmos-phere inside the house which enables the smoke to hang in the air for a longer amount of time. Spraying the lower regions with water can be beneficial in achieving this but care should be taken to keep the foliage dry.

*White Fly*

Again this pest breeds at an alarming rate. Its presence is usually revealed only when the plant is handled or disturbed, when the adult fly take off for a short flight only to return or settle on a nearby plant.

In common with aphids, this pest excretes a sticky deposit which can be seen on the upper surface of a leaf below that of the host leaf. For control Malathion, Resmithrin or Lindane can again be used.

*Aphids*

These pests often go unobserved until large colonies have built up. They breed and multiply at a terrific rate, and the injury to plants as a result of their feeding habits distorts growth and foliage. Other effects of heavy aphid infestation are the attraction of ants to the honeydew excreted by the aphids, and the growth of sooty moulds on these deposits, giving the plant a very dirty appearance.

Aphids can in addition carry viruses, but fortunately the fuchsia seems to have a built-in resistance to these.

Effective control can be obtained with Malathion or Lindane.

*Red Spider Mite*

The presence of this pest will indicate immediately that growing conditions in the greenhouse are completely adverse to those required by fuchsias. The mite flourishes only under hot, dry conditions and, if allowed, will quickly spread throughout the house. If it is not detected in the early stages, plants can be defoliated in a very short time. Red spider are difficult to detect with the naked eye, but their presence is indicated by the underside of the leaf turning a brownish colour and eventual leaf fall.

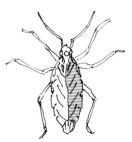

Figure 7.1
The More
Common Pests

Control of this pest is most effective by the use of a systemic insecticide, or for mild attacks a Malathion spray or aerosol, and Derris.

The grower should ensure that future attacks do not occur by providing a shading against hot sunshine and frequent sprays of clear water to the greenhouse benches and floor to promote a moist atmosphere.

### Capsid Bug

Two species of this pest exist, the common green capsid bug and the tarnished plant bug. The damage they do is identical, both attacking fresh, young growing tips, causing malformed growth or in many cases blind shoots. In addition to this they also attack young flower buds. Both are similar in size and have a body like an oversized aphid, although they fly only occasionally when disturbed.

Control is not difficult if a regular spray programme is carried out. Malathion, Pyrethrum and Lindane are very effective.

### Thrips

This pest in its nymph stage is very difficult to detect, not simply because it is so very small but also because at that stage its body is transparent. The adult thrip when closely examined can be likened to a narrow-bodied ant and although only approximately one-sixteenth of an inch long can readily be seen on the underside of leaves or on flowers. At first sight they can be mistaken for soot smuts. Severe attacks can cripple growing points and flowers. For control, one can use Pyrethrum, Lindane or Malathion.

### Leaf Hopper

This is a very active pest which will take flying leaps to safety when disturbed. Under the protected conditions of the greenhouse they will breed continuously. Serious attacks by this pest produce a characteristic mottling of leaves and eventually retard active growth. It is in the nymph stage that this damage is done, so that preventative sprays are a wise precaution.

Control: Malathion or Lindane.

### Vine Weevil

Attacks by this beetle-like insect are not a serious threat to fuchsia

109

growers in general but on occasion it has been known to cause problems for some growers. Usually the first signs that the beetle is present is the damage to the leaf, which will have small pieces eaten from it, usually at the edge, by the adult. The grub of this beetle is invariably found in the soil ball where it feeds on the roots of the plant and if allowed to go unchecked will eventually cause the complete collapse of the plant. Control of this beetle and its grub is by a systemic insecticide and routine greenhouse hygiene, removing all decaying plant material.

*Fungoid Disease*

Most horticulturists will be familiar with the grey mould fungus *Botrytis cinerea* which occurs on all kinds of rotting vegetation and fruits. It is probably the greatest threat and enemy to greenhouse culture.

Young plants and cuttings become easy prey to a fungoid disease in houses that are badly ventilated, cold and damp. Other contributary factors are overcrowding and lack of general cleanliness, of pots, trays, staging or flooring.

Plants in early growth are particularly susceptible to attack in houses with excessive moisture. It can cause rotting of stems and leaves and will quickly spread throughout the house.

The only effective control of this disease is the maintenance of correct growing conditions. First and foremost airy conditions must be provided, heating should be kept to a level that will enable growth to continue evenly, moisture must be controlled and the house kept clean. Routine inspection of plants and prompt destruction of plants that are suspect is advised. Some measure of control against fungoid diseases is always worthwhile even if offending plants have been removed and growing conditions have been corrected.

There are a number of fungicides available such a lime-sulphur or those based on copper or thiram. Many makers of pest control preparations now market combined chemical agents to kill mites and both sucking and biting pests. Other preparations combine insecticides and fungicides.

Almost always it will be found that certain chemicals react unfavourably to some plant species. Fortunately the fuchsia is not one of them, but if other exotic plants are grown in the same house the instructions should always be read carefully before use.

*Rust*

This disease fortunately is rarely seen on the fuchsia and then possibly only in areas where the rosebay willow herb is growing, from which source the spore is produced. Infected plants can be identified by the presence of orangey coloured pustules under the leaves. All infected leaves should be removed and burnt. Spray plants with zineb or thiram at weekly intervals for a period of several weeks.

# CHAPTER 8

# Fuchsias in the Garden

Among the many thousands of fuchsais available there are many hardy species and cultivars suitable for garden decoration. These can be planted directly into position and, over the years, will develop into quite large bushes and hedges. Care should be taken when planting fuchsias that are intended to remain in the open ground throughout the winter, to provide a well drained site, as waterlogged ground can be as fatal as a hard frost. All plants that are to overwinter in outside positions must be planted at least 2 in deeper than the level of the pot soil, to afford additional protection to the lower stem and roots. No attempt to prune established plants should be made before all danger of frosts is over, as this also assists in protecting the lower parts of the plant. In the spring, when new growth begins, it may be found after a particularly hard winter that the old top growth has succumbed to the weather. Such plants should be allowed to remain in position as many fuchsias will produce new growth from below soil level, at which time the old growth should be removed.

The classification of many fuchsias as hardy would depend upon where in Britian the plants were grown. Winter conditions in the north might well be too severe for some of these so-called hardy varieties, but there is not much else one can do except test and try out several varieties of this type and build up one's own local knowledge. A visit to your nearest specialist fuchsia nurseryman will no doubt prove helpful in this respect.

In the south, winter conditions are less severe and many of the so-called tender varieties have survived the average winter along with the hardies.

Planting fuchsias in their pots directly into a display bed is a technique employed by some gardeners as this facilitates easy removal in the autumn, in those areas subject to the more severe winter conditions. Plants used in this way do have a certain root restriction because of the pot, although it may well be found that the roots have penetrated the drainage holes of the pot and will need to be trimmed off before being returned to the greenhouse or frame for overwintering. If this method is employed, it is essential that a good sized pot be used and, when planting, that the pot is completely covered by the soil surface. A mulch of peat over the entire bed will not only improve the appearance of the bed as a whole but will help to conserve moisture, a point that needs to be watched carefully.

Standards and half standards are plant forms often used for garden decoration, and these are cases where the in-pot, in-bed system can be used to advantage. The very nature of the varieties used for this plant form is one of vigour and this includes the root system. Therefore an adequate pot size is of the utmost importance as a well grown standard might have a head some 3 ft in diameter and it should not be taken for granted that adventitious roots will automatically seek sustenance outside the container. Plants of this dimension must be securely staked. If at all possible the stake should be pushed through the drainage hole of the pot into the soil below and the other end must support the entire height of the plant, finishing approximately ½ in below the top layer of leaves. It is advisable to have at least two ties in the depth of head and several more up the stem. A plant that may be worth £10 or more and taken two or more years work to achieve, deserves this attention for it could be ruined in no time at all.

For general garden cultivation the bush or shrub shape is normally favoured, and this is encouraged by removing the growing tip to allow side shoots to develop. These in turn are pinched out after two pairs of leaves have developed on each side growth. For the first year's growth this is normally sufficient to produce a nice bushy plant, but a lot will depend on the vigour of each variety. More ambitious shapes are described under training.

It is prudent to ensure that the pots used for plunging into outside beds be of the clay variety and not plastic.

Fuchsia hardiness trials have been conducted extensively over many years now and, as a result of collective data received, the BFS has recommended a selected list of cultivars and species as hardy. This is primarily for the purpose of show bench definition. However, although this may appear to be a somewhat cautious recommendation, much depending on geographical location, there is every reason to expect satisfactory results if the proposed permanent bedding site is well prepared and in a position offering some protection from the weather.

**Hardy Fuchsias**

Preparation of the plot to be cultivated is normally carried out during the autumn months, when deep digging to break up solidly compacted soil and to improve drainage is best achieved. It should then be left rough throughout the winter to weather. The addition of composted garden refuse or well rotted manure, liberally forked in during the process, will not only improve the physical structure of the soil but increase the depth of fertile root run, an essential factor for ensuring success in permanent plantings.

Exposure to frost, snow, rain and drying winds generally break up the surface and with the approach of warmer weather and spring sunshine the improved texture of the soil will be noticed by the ease of raking down the rough surface to a fine tilth.

Plants selected, whether purchased or raised oneself, should be grown on in pots and hardened off in a cold frame before being planted out in the garden site. This should not be attempted until all danger of frost is past, as the aim now is to get them off to a good start without a check.

A planting technique usefully employed is to scoop out a shallow hole 12 in in diameter and approximately 3 in deep. In the centre of this, dig out a second hole of sufficient size to receive the root ball, place in position and firm well in. When well established and growing strongly, fill in the shallow hole and level off, to afford extra protection to the root system from freezing conditions.

These preliminary preparations may be thought to be over-fastidious, but with fuchsias the borderline between hardy and tender is very narrow, and in some cases failure to survive can be attributed more to inadequate protection and careless planting than adverse weather conditions. Here then is the recommended list of fuchsias with a known potential to survive the average winter.

*Abbé Farges* French 1901. Semi-double; tube and sepals pale-cerise; corolla lilac. Flowers small but very profuse. Growth upright and bushy; foliage small and sturdy. An excellent choice for small pot culture, but will also achieve larger dimensions if required and is often exhibited in 6 in pots.

*Abundance* British 1870. Single; tube and sepals cerise; corolla purple with cerise petaloids. Flowers of medium size and produced freely on vigorous bushy spreading growth. Award of Merit RHS Hardy Trials 1975-78. This cultivar should not be confused with that of the same name raised by Niederholzer in America in 1944.

*Achievement* British 1886. Single; tube and sepals cerise; corolla purple. Flower medium to large, profuse and of good shape. The light green foliage is the perfect foil to beautiful flowers. Among the best of British introductions, very easy to grow and will respond to any desired growth form.

*Admiration* British 1940. Single; tube and sepals cherry red; corolla deep crimson. Flowers medium sized and slender. Growth lax bush.

*Alice Hoffman* German 1911. Semi-double; tube and sepals rose; corolla white. Flower and foliage small; growth upright and compact. Ideal for small pot culture.

*A.M. Larwick* New Zealand 1940. Tube and sepals rich carmine; corolla purple to mauve. The medium flowers are freely produced. Foliage is a medium green with red centre vein. Growth upright and bushy. Suitable for most forms of upright growth.

*Army Nurse* American 1947. Semi-double; tube and sepals carmine; corolla violet veined and flushed carmine at base. Flowers small but very freely produced. Growth strong, upright and vigorous. Suitable as bush or standard.

*Avalanche* British 1869. Double; tube and sepals scarlet; corolla purple with carmine flush at the base. Flowers medium to large, foliage citrine-green. Growth tending to lax, suitable for an open bush and basket work.

*Bashful* British 1974. Double; tube and sepals deep pink, corolla white veined red. Flower small but freely produced on stiff, strong bushy growth which attains a height of about 12 inches. Foliage deep green. Award of Merit, RHS Hardy Trials 1975-78.

*Beacon* British 1871. Single; tube and sepals deep pink; corolla mauvish-pink. A medium sized flower is freely produced on compact upright bushy growth. Foliage of dark green with waved edge. Highly Commended, RHS Hardy Trials 1975-78.

*Beranger* French 1882. Double; tube and sepals deep red; corolla violet. Flowers medium sized. Growth low and lax.

*Blue Bonnet* British 1974. Double; tube and sepals red; corolla dark blue. The flower of medium size is very freely produced on upright, bushy growth. Foliage dark green. Award of Merit, RHS Hardy Trials 1975-78. (This cultivar should not be confused with that of the same name raised by Hodges in America in 1950.)

*Blue Gown* British (date unknown). Double; tube and sepals cerise; corolla bluish-purple splashed pink and carmine. Large flower. Growth vigorous and upright. Will produce both bush and standard forms quite easily.

*Bouquet* French 1893. Single, tube and sepals red; corolla violet. Flowers small and very freely produced. Growth low bush.

*Brilliant* British 1865. Single; tube and sepals scarlet; corolla violet magenta veined red. Flower medium and very freely produced. Growth vigorous upright and bushy, requires to be frequently pinched for bush growth, but does also make an excellent standard.

*Caledonia* French 1899. Single, tube and sepals cerise, corolla crimson. Flowers medium and freely produced. Growth strong upright bush but will make a neat low hedge.

*Cardinal Farges* British 1958. Semi-double; tube and sepals pale cerise, corolla white veined cerise. The small flowers are profuse. Growth upright bushy and vigorous, foliage small. A mutation from Abbé Farges.

*Carmen* French 1893. Semi-double; tube and sepals cerise, corolla purple. Flower small but very profuse. Growth dwarf and upright, one of the best of its kind.

*Carnea* British 1861. Single; tube and sepals scarlet; corolla purple. Flowers small and freely produced, foliage small. Growth dwarf and upright.

*Charming* British 1895. Single; tube and sepals carmine; corolla reddish purple. Very free medium flowers, foliage light green. Growth of medium height and bushy.

*Chillerton Beauty* British 1847. Single; tube and sepals light rose-pink; corolla violet mauve. Flowers small, but freely produced. Growth upright bush, suitable for a hedge.

116

*C. J. Howlett* British 1911. Single; tube and sepals reddish pink tipped green; corolla bluish-carmine. Flowers small and freely produced. Growth is upright and bushy. An ideal subject for bedding work. Award of Merit, RHS Hardy Trials 1975-78.

*Cliffs Hardy* British 1966. Single, tube and sepals crimson tipped green; corolla violet, paling at base and veined scarlet. Flowers are medium sized and held high, freely produced. Growth vigorous bush.

*Conspicua* British 1863. Single; tube and sepals scarlet; corolla white veined scarlet. Flowers small but very freely produced. Growth neat and bushy.

*Constance* American 1935. Double; tube and sepals pink; corolla mauve with pink coloration. Flowers medium sized and free. Growth upright and bushy.

*Corallina* British 1844. Single; tube and sepals scarlet; corolla rich purple. Flowers medium and free. Growth vigorous and spreading, suitable as a hedge or a bush.

*David* British 1937. Single, tube and sepals cerise; corolla rich red-purple. Flowers small and free. Growth short upright bush.

*Display* British 1881. Single, tube and sepals rose-pink; corolla dusky pink. Flowers medium sized and very profuse. The corolla is displayed firmly and is very attractively reminiscent of a coolie's hat in shape. Growth strong and upright and, being self-branching, will respond to any plant form desired. 1881 to 1979 and still a great favourite for the show bench.

*Doctor Foster* French 1899. Single; tube and sepals scarlet; corolla violet. Flowers large and free. Growth upright bush, has been used successfully as a low hedge.

*Dorothy* British 1946. Single; tube and sepals brilliant crimson; corolla violet with red veining. Flowers medium and free. Growth upright bush or a low hedge.

*Drame* French 1880. Semi-double; tube and sepals scarlet; corolla violet-purple. Flowers small to medium and free. Growth upright and bushy.

*Dunrobin Bedder* British 1890. Single; tube and sepals scarlet; corolla dark-purple. Freely produced small flowers on dwarf and spreading growth, an ideal subject for the rockery.

*El Cid* British 1966. Single; tube and sepals deep-red; corolla rich-burgandy. Flowers medium sized and freely produced on upright growth. Will make a well-balanced bush.

*Eleanor Rawlins* British 1954. Single; tube and sepals carmine; corolla hunting-pink paling at base. Flowers small but produced in great profusion. Growth upright, compact and bushy.

*Elfin Glade* British 1963. Single; tube and sepals rose-pink, corolla mauve with pink casts and veining. Flowers medium sized and free. Growth is bushy.

*Empress of Prussia* British 1868. Single; tube and sepals rich-scarlet; corolla warm magenta paling at base. Flowers medium but produced severally at each flower-producing axil. Growth bushy and extremely vigorous.

*Enfante Prodigue* French 1887. Semi-double; tube and sepals crimson; corolla rich blue-purple. Flowers medium and free. Growth upright and bushy.

*Flash* American (date unknown). Single; tube and sepals red to light magenta with corolla of similar colouring, almost a self. Foliage small and profuse and of light green colouring. Growth vigorous bush, makes an excellent show plant.

*Florence Turner* British 1955. Single; tube pale pink, sepals white; corolla pale purple. Flowers medium sized. Growth upright and bushy.

*Florian* French 1897. Single; tube and sepals coral pink; corolla violet mauve. Flowers small and slender, very free. Growth upright bush.

*Genii* American 1951. Single; tube and sepals cerise; corolla rich violet ageing to dark rose. Flowers small and profuse. Foliage an attractive yellowish-green with red stems. Growth upright and bushy.

*Glow* British 1946. Single; tube and sepals cerise; corolla scarlet at base overlaid purple. Flowers small and free. Growth low and bushy.

118

*Graf Witte* French 1899. Single; tube and sepals light-scarlet; corolla mauve, shading through rose to purple. Flowers small and very free. Foliage yellowish-green with red veining. Growth upright and bushy.

*Herald* British 1887. Single, tube and sepals scarlet; corolla dark purple. Flowers of medium size with recurving sepals. Growth upright and bushy.

*H.G. Brown* British 1946. Single; tube and sepals deep-scarlet; corolla deep-lake. Flower smallish but profuse. Foliage dark-green with a glossy sheen. Growth low and bushy.

*Howletts Hardy* British 1952. Single; tube and sepals deep scarlet; corolla violet to purple with scarlet veining. Flowers medium to large. Growth bushy, will attain a height of approximately 2 ft in outside conditions.

*Immaculate* British 1940. Single; tube and sepals rich-red shaded orange glow; corolla deeper shade of red. Flowers medium sized and free. Foliage dark-green with a glossy sheen. Growth upright and bushy.

*Isabel Ryan* British 1974. Single; tube and sepals red, corolla white veined pink. Flowers of medium size are freely produced and contrast well against dark green foliage. Growth upright and bushy will reach a height of 2 feet. Award of Merit, RHS Hardy Trials 1975-78.

*Jewel* British 1940. Single; tube and sepals carmine; corolla purple. Flower long and slender. Growth upright and bushy.

*Joan Cooper* British 1953. Single; tube and sepals rose-blush; corolla bright cherry-red. Flower small but profuse, with acutely reflexed sepal formation. Growth vigorous, upright and bushy. Foliage tends to light-green. When introduced by W.P. Wood was regarded as a definite colour break in the hardy section.

*John* British 1946. Single; tube and sepals crimson; corolla deep-lilac. Flower small and freely produced. Growth dwarf, ideal rockery subject.

*Kathleen* British 1940. Single; tube and sepals cerise tipped green on sepal points; corolla rose-pink. Flowers very small but profuse. Growth erect though dwarf. This cultivar should not be mistaken for Kathleen raised by Pugh 1974.

*Lady Thumb* British 1966. Semi-double; tube and sepals light carmine; corolla white veined carmine. Flower and foliage small. Growth upright though dwarf. A mutation from Tom Thumb.

*Lena* British 1862. Semi-double; tube and sepals flesh-pink, sepal underside deeper-pink; corolla rose-magenta with pink flush. Flowers of medium size freely produced. Sometimes used for basket culture when its lax growth is used to advantage. Also very popular for outside permanent planting.

*Liebriez* German 1874. Semi-double; tube and sepals pale-cerise; corolla pinky-white with pink veining. Flower small but freely produced over a long period. Growth upright and bushy. Very often seen as a specimen plant in a 5 in pot on the show bench.

*Lottie Hobby* British 1839. Single; tube and sepals scarlet; corolla a brighter scarlet. Flower very small but freely produced. Foliage also very small with glossy sheen. Growth upright though dwarf. A species hybrid from the Encliandra section.

*Margaret* British 1943. Semi-double; tube and sepals carmine; corolla wood-violet with cerise veining. Flowers medium sized and very free. Growth vigorous, upright and bushy. Good for hedge work.

*Margaret Brown* British 1949. Single; tube and sepals rose-pink; corolla pale rose-bengal. Flowers small but freely produced. Foliage lightish-green. Growth upright and bushy.

*Mme Cornelissen* Belgian 1860. Semi-double; tube and sepals rich-scarlet; corolla white with cerise veining. Flowers long and slender, very free. Growth vigorous, upright and bushy.

*Margery Blake* British 1950. Single; tube and sepals scarlet; corolla purple. Flower small and produced freely and continuously to autumn. Growth upright and bushy.

*Mary Thorne* British 1954. Single; tube and sepals turkey-red; corolla violet. Flowers medium and very free. Growth vigorous, upright bush.

*Miniature* French 1894. Single; tube and sepals cerise; corolla purple. Flowers small and freely produced. Growth dwarf and rather lax.

*Minos* French 1902. Semi-double; tube and sepals scarlet; corolla purple with magenta veining. Flowers medium sized and free. Growth upright to arching.

*Mrs Popple* British 1899. Single; tube and sepals scarlet; corolla violet with cerise veining. Flowers medium sized and freely produced. Growth vigorous upright bush. Used frequently for hedging.

*Mrs W.P. Wood* British 1949. Single; tube and sepals pale-pink; corolla white. Flowers small, produced freely. Foliage small. Growth very vigorous and rampant. Flowers could be likened to *Magellanica alba* for colour and form, but this cultivar produces flowers nearly twice the size.

*Mr A. Huggett* British (date unknown). Single; tube and sepals cerise; corolla mauve-pink, petals edged lilac-magenta. Flowers medium to small and very free. Growth upright and bushy.

*Nicola Jane* British 1959. Double; tube and sepals cerise; corolla blush-pink suffused and veined cerise. Flowers medium sized and freely produced. Growth is upright and bushy, responds well to training.

*Norma* French 1896. Double; tube and sepals red; corolla deep-lavender. Flowers small and free but produced in flushes tending to sparse as season progresses. Growth dwarf.

*Papoose* American 1960. Semi-double; tube and sepals bright-red; corolla dark-purple. Flowers small and extremely profuse. Growth bush. Will respond to training.

*Pee Wee Rose* American 1959. Semi-double; tube and sepals rosy-red; corolla pale rose. Flowers small but produced in great profusion. Foliage small on willowy growth. Award of Merit, RHS Hardy Trials 1975-78.

*Peggy King* British 1954. Single; tube and sepals rich rose-red; corolla purple, smallish flowers are produced freely. Growth upright and bushy. Can be used to good effect as a hedging subject.

*Phyllis* British 1938. Semi double; tube and sepals rose, corolla deep-rose. Flowers small to medium and produced freely over a long season. Growth very vigorous and stiffly upright. An ideal choice for producing standards and pillars in double quick time, or for a quick hedge.

*Pixie* British 1960. Single; tube and sepals scarlet; corolla mauve veined scarlet. Flowers small and very freely produced. Foliage light-green. Growth upright and very vigorous.

*Phoenix* French 1913. Semi-double; tube and sepals carmine; corolla purple highlighted cerise. Flower medium to large and free. Growth upright and bushy.

*President* British 1841. Single; tube and sepals bright-red; corolla rose-magenta. Flowers medium sized and freely produced. Foliage dark-green. Growth vigorous upright bush.

*Profusion* British 1938. Single; tube and sepals scarlet; corolla violet to purple. Smallish flower freely produced. Growth upright slender fronds, gradually arching, bushy.

*Prostrata* British 1841. Single; tube and sepals red; corolla violet. Flowers very small. Growth prostrate and fast spreading, suitable for rockery work.

*Pumila* British 1821. Single; tube and sepals bright-red; corolla mauve. Flowers small and profuse. Growth low, upright and bushy. Ideal rockery plant.

*Purple Cornelissen* Belgian 1897. Single; tube and sepals cerise; corolla purple. Flowers medium sized and freely produced. Growth upright and bushy.

*Purple Splendour* British 1974. Double; tube and sepals crimson; corolla bluish-purple. Growth though strong is of somewhat spreading habit to a height of 2 feet. Introduced by Sunningdale Nurseries, who state that the flower is often confused with that of Prodigy, the correct name of which is Enfante Prodigue. Highly Commended, RHS Hardy Trials 1975-78.

*Rhombifolia* French 1870. Single; tube and sepals cerise; corolla purple. Flowers small and very freely produced. Growth upright and free branching.

*Ronsard* French 1897. Single; tube and sepals cerise; corolla violet purple. Flower small and freely produced. Growth upright and bushy.

*Robin Hood* British 1966. Double; tube and sepals bright-red; corolla dark crimson. Flower largish and free. Growth upright and bushy. A very strong-stemmed cultivar most suitable for outside work.

*Rose of Castile* British 1855. Single; tube and sepals waxy-white with green-tipped sepal points; corolla purple flushed pale rose fading at base. Flower small to medium freely produced. Growth upright and bushy.

*Rose of Castile Improved* British 1869. Single; tube and sepals flesh-pink; corolla violet-purple. Flowers of medium size and fairly free. Growth upright and bushy. A good old reliable type for a permanent outside planting.

*Rufus* American 1952. Single; A glowing turkey-red self. Flower of medium size and produced freely. Strong upright growth. Award of Merit, RHS Hardy Trials 1975-78.

*Ruth* British 1949. Single; tube and sepals red; corolla purple. Flower of medium size and free. Growth upright and bushy.

*Santa Cruz* American 1947. Semi-double; tube and sepals deep crimson; corolla darker crimson. Large flower is produced freely. Growth upright and bushy. Highly Commended, RHS Hardy Trials 1975-78.

*Scarcity* British 1869. Single; tube and sepals cerise; corolla rosy-purple. Flowers of medium size and free. Growth upright and bushy. Another good old cultivar that will pleasantly surprise.

*Sharpitor* British 1974. Single; tube and sepals scarlet; corolla mauve-pink. Flower small, but freely produced. The foliage is also small, but attractively variegated cream and pale green. This cultivar is a mutation of Mrs W. P. Wood. Highly Commended, RHS Hardy Trials 1975-78.

*Silverdale* British 1962. Single; tube ivory, and rather short; sepals longish, eau-de-nil flushed pale-pink tipped green; corolla lavender. Flowers small and freely produced. Foliage pale green. Growth upright and bushy.

*Susan Travis* British 1958. Single; tube and sepals deep-pink; corolla rose-pink. Flowers medium sized and produced freely. Growth strong and upright with free branching habit. Produces a fine showy display of colour.

*Telegraph* French 1886. Single; tube and sepals red; corolla purple. Flowers small and freely produced. Growth upright and bushy.

*Tennessee Waltz* American 1951. Semi-double; tube and sepals rose madder; corolla lilac-lavender flushed rose. A medium sized flower of squarish shape, with upswept petals. Flower is freely produced. A self branching plant of strong upright growth. Award of Merit, RHS Hardy Trials 1975-78.

*The Tarns* British 1962. Single; tube short, sepals long, pale-pink; corolla violet-blue. Flowers medium very freely produced. Growth upright and bushy.

*Tom Thumb* French 1850. Single; tube and sepals carmine-red, corolla mauve with carmine veining. Flowers very small and profuse. Growth upright dwarf bush, suitable for rockeries.

*Trase* British 1959. Double; tube and sepals cerise; corolla white with cerise veining. Flowers medium sized and profuse. Growth upright bushy and compact.

*Tresco* Single; tube and sepals red; corolla purple. Flowers small and very free. Growth vigorous spreading bush.

*Tricolorii* British (Date unknown). Single; tube and sepals crimson; corolla purple. Flower small and very free. Very attractive variegated foliage, green and cream flushed pink. Growth upright to arching and bushy. Suitable for hedging to about 3 ft.

*Trudy* British 1969. Single; tube and sepals rhodamine-pink; corolla cyclamen-pink. A small bell shaped flower with sharply reflexing sepals is freely produced. Growth is bushy and upright. Highly Commended, RHS Hardy Trials 1975-78.

*White Pixie* British 1968. Single; tube and sepals reddish carmine; corolla white veined pink; attractive yellow-green foliage with red veins. Flowers medium to small. Growth upright to arching. A good plant for outdoor work, can be used for low hedgework. A mutation from Pixie, which was a mutation from Graf Witte. White Pixie does occasionally revert, and has been known to show characteristics of all three.

*W.P. Wood* British 1954. Single; tube and sepals scarlet; corolla violet blue. Flowers small to medium and freely produced. Growth upright and bushy.

*F. bacillaris* Mexico, Lindley 1832. (*Breviflorae* section *Encliandra*) Tube and sepals red; corolla rose. Flower tiny, foliage small. Growth upright, vigorous and self-branching.

*F. coccinea* Brazil or Chile, 1788. Tube and sepals red; corolla purple. Flowers gracefully slender and attractive. The first species to be introduced into England. (*Quelusia* section).

*F. hemsleyana* Costa Rica and Panama 1937. (*Breviflorae* section *Encliandra*). A rose-coloured self, minute flower, growth tall, shrubby and attractive.

*F. magellanica* Chile and Argentina 1768. (*Quelusia* section). Tube red, sepals deep red; corolla purple. Flowers are elegant, graceful and of classic form, growth strong and vigorous, produces numerous auxiliary growths from below soil level. The flowers are borne profusely on its long slender arching stems. This species once established will flourish in the wildest conditions, and can often be seen forming hedges in many parts of the British Isles.

*F. magellanica var. Molinae* (synonymous Alba) Tube white; corolla very pale lilac. Very hardy and will in time attain a height of 10 ft.

*F. magellanica var. Discolor* Tube and sepals red; corolla mauve. Growth dwarf.

*F. magellanica var. Gracilis* Tube and sepals red; corolla deep mauve. Rampant arching growth.

*F. magellanica var. Gracilis Variegata* Identical to above but with silver variegated foliage.

*F. magellanica var. Longipedunculata* Tube and sepals red; corolla lilac-mauve. Flowers long and slender.

*F. magellanica var. Macrostemma* Tube red, sepals lighter red; corolla mauve. Flowers slightly longer than type. Growth strong and upright.

*F. magellanica var. Riccartonii* Tube and sepals scarlet; corolla deep-purple. Growth and the abundance of flower make this hybrid the more popular of choice for spectacular hedges or bush.

*F. magellanica var. Globosa* Tube and sepals scarlet; corolla purple. Flowers as name indicates are more globular than type. Growth strong and robust.

*F. magellanica var. Thompsonii* Tube and sepals scarlet; corolla purple. Flowers small but more slender. Growth upright to arching, perhaps a little too open and loose.

The following cultivars, previously described, also received awards at the RHS Hardy Trials 1975-78.

### First Class Certificate

*Lady Thumb*
*F. magellanica var. Riccartonii*
*Mme Cornelissen*

### Award of Merit

*Chillerton Beauty*
*Cliff's Hardy*
*F. magellanica var. Gracilis Variegata*
*Graf Witte*
*F. magellanica var. Gracilis*
*Trase*
*Ruth*

### Highly Commended

*Pixie*
*Susan Travis*

# CHAPTER 9

# Amateur Fuchsia Breeding

This must be the most rewarding of all garden activities, and one that any amateur with a knowledge and ability to recognise a good fuchsia plant can pursue.

The choice of parents is ultimately dictated by individual perception and anticipation. Any first experiment is basically a fact finding exercise to establish the promising parents for future experiment, and it follows that siblings derived from good parents may also become good parents. The novice hybridiser can and frequently does produce new varieties of outstanding merit from nothing more than an inspired hunch.

Only by experimental crosses can any breeding programme be started, and the only possible advise to a would-be hybridiser is the obvious need to select parents from among personal favourite cultivars displaying health, vigour and freedom of flower.

Artificial pollination of the fuchsia is really very simple and requires no complicated technique other than a process called emasculation. Like most other flowers, the fuchsia has both stamens and pistil and can, if allowed, fertilise itself. This possibility must therefore be prevented by recourse to emasculation, ie., removal of the stamens. Select the flower to be emasculated when it is about to open naturally. Open the flower fully and remove the stamens, a simple operation with a pair of small scissors. Some difficulty may be experienced if fully double flowers restrict the complete emergence of all anthers. In this case several petals (or even all) may also be carefully removed (see Figure 9.2).

Pollen from the male member must be fresh, and is best transferred to the prepared flower by taking an anther with its pollen and applying it directly to the stigma.

Positive adherence of the pollen must be observed, as the young stigma is not fully receptive at this early stage. Provided the pollen is deposited on the stigma, germination will proceed when the stigma is ripe.

Figure 9.1 (left)
Parts of the
Fuchsia Flower

Figure 9.2 (right)
Emasculated
Flower

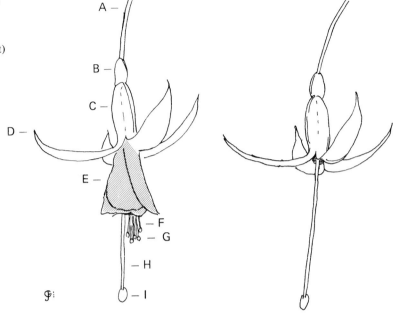

A. Pedicel
B. Ovary
C. Tube (Hypanthium)
D. Sepal
E. Petals (Corolla)

F. Stamen
G. Anther
H. Style
I. Stigma

Rapid and successful germination is governed to a large extent by favourable temperature, 70-75°F being the ideal range for optimum success. It can be effective within an hour.

The pollinated flower must be given protection against foreign pollen drifting or being carried by visiting insects. This is usually done by enclosing the whole flower within a nylon or muslin bag until such time as the flower drops, to leave the remaining fruit to ripen. Bags for this purpose can be made from old nylon curtains or tights, etc. Not all crosses are successful — that is part of the hybridiser's lot. Most failures are due to the inability of a pollen tube to find the right organic nutrients it needs to sustain continuous growth down the style to the embryo sac, where fertilisation and subsequent development take place.

Crosses between two plants in which the roles of male and female are reversed — reciprocal crosses — are sometimes practiced by hybridisers, but it makes no difference to the characters bestowed on the siblings. The only advantage of this practice is pollen germination which is sometimes more effective one way than the other, and

128

for this reason it is perhaps worth trying the procedure.

Several different crosses should be made primarily to find the best parents and to observe the distribution of parental characteristics among the siblings of each cross.

Keep a record of each cross made. The conventional method is to enter the female parent, followed by the sign ♀ then the male parent and sign ♂ and the date. The results of each cross can be identified by any method convenient to the individual.

A slight shrivelling of the fruit skin will indicate a suitable time to harvest the seed. This can be done efficiently either by direct extraction or by squashing the fruit in a saucer of water. Remove fleshy fruit and skin and gather viable seeds to the sides of the saucer. These will be identified by their sinking to the bottom: useless seed husks will float.

Make sure all viable seed is thoroughly air dried before packeting and storage, to await the earliest opportunity to sow. The practice of sowing seed as soon as it is harvested has little to commend itself in terms of economy in space involved and high winter fuel costs. Indeed any advantage gained by so doing is not apparent in the end result.

If seed is sown and given an early start by use of the propagating bench, when rooting cuttings in the first months of the year, they can be raised and nurtured into full flower production in the current season. Most seeds sown from late winter to early spring will flower the first year although it may on occasion be found that an odd plant will need to be overwintered to the next season. This is rare, but has been known to happen.

If sowings are to be made in wooden seed trays, they should be thoroughly scrubbed clean and then rinsed in clean water containing a mild disinfectant before filling with compost. Firm the compost lightly and level off to within ½ in of the top. At this point the compost should be watered, using a fine rose attachment on the can, and then set aside to drain off before sowing the seed thinly over the surface. The seed should then be covered by sieving a layer of compost over them. This should be of a depth that is approximately the same as the diameter of the seed. Place onto the propagating bench and cover with a sheet of glass to prevent excessive moisture loss and the possible need of a further watering. The glass must be turned each morning and evening and can be dispensed with entirely once positive germination is seen.

Limited sowings can be undertaken in seed pans. The clay variety are ideal if one is fortunate to have these available, but they seem to be practically non-existent at the moment, so the next best thing is to use plastic pot saucers, which can, if one feels that it is necessary have several holes drilled through the bottom to facilitate drainage.

It might be found that the holes are unnecessary, in which case they will still be serviceable for their original purpose. A useful tip when using this type of pan is, instead of covering with a piece of glass as one would normally do, simply invert another pan of the same size and place over the top. Care must be taken to inspect each day and remove excess moisture. As soon as the seed is seen to be germinating, remove the top pan completely.

An alternative which is particularly useful for individual sowing when there is a need to tabulate each seedling, is the use of multipot trays. Such trays eliminate root disturbance when potting-on.

Seed sown in pans or trays must be pricked out as soon as they can be easily handled, directly into thumb-sized pots or, if the quantity makes individual potting impracticable, into deeper boxes, spacing each seedling approximately 2 in apart each way.

Whatever method is used, the parentage of each seedling should be clearly identified by some system of marking.

The seedlings having been moved on into fresh compost must be lightly watered and kept in a warm, damp atmosphere for a day or two and shaded against sudden periods of sunshine that could cause distress or serious wilting.

Any move to cooler greenhouse conditions will be dependent on how quickly the seedlings recover and settle in. The signs of this will be obvious to the observant. Subsequent treatment will follow the usual potting-on procedures as growth develops, and each plant can be stopped once, at three pairs of leaves to encourage early lateral growth.

Harden the plants off in a cold frame before planting out in the trial bed to flower and await your critical assessment. Instant success has been known, but accept it as a rare possibility only. Look over and make careful choice of sibling plants showing some promise of desired characteristics and consider the desirability of crossing back to either parent or among the siblings themselves. The results could be fascinating and certainly educational.

The ancestry of the fuchsias used by today's hybridisers are very mixed up due to the extensive crossings by the early pioneer breeders and, using these multi-hybrids, one can only anticipate in a very general sense the results of any given cross. However, an understanding of the basic laws of inheritance will provide an intelligible approach to the art of breeding.

Gregor Mendel's work and perception gave the world two simple laws. The first is that when two pure bred individuals displaying a pair of contrasting characters are crossed, the original parental characters are recovered in half of the second filial generation (F2), the remainder being of hybrid constitution. The first filial generation (F1) will all be hybrid, displaying a condition intermediate between the two parents, or having one of the characters (the 'recessive') obscured by the other (the 'dominant').

The second law is that when several pairs of contrasting characters are crossed they segregate independently of each other. Quite simply, characters from either parent pass at random to any of their siblings. Later research has slightly modified this assertion, in that characters located on the same chromosome are usually inherited together.

Despite this, it can be seen that the possibilities of crossing among the siblings or even back to either parent must present the raiser with a better than even chance of extracting and combining the desired qualities of both parents.

Today's raisers are at a particular disadvantage in that the parents of any given cross they make between hybrids, are already the end result of very mixed parentage and any of their offspring can exhibit some trait of their forebears in quite disconcerting ways. Others will be to a greater or lesser degree more closely related to their immediate parents, and it is these that the raiser will either self-pollinate, back cross to either parent or among the siblings themselves in the hope of embodying the best factors of both parents in one or other of the resultant progeny.

Conflicting characters, such as long jointed stems and short jointed stems, are to be avoided if a short internodal length of stem is required, for many wasters would be produced. Similarly, if single flowers are required one would only use single flowered parents in their crosses and conversly double flowered parents would be used for producing double flowered progeny.

Many breeders like to think that a particular flower colour is the end result of a planned colour mix, as on a painter's pallet, but this is a fallacy. Colour development does not follow the law of physics, for if white is the sum total of all colours, we would be able to extract all the colours of the rainbow. Plants are a law unto themselves and, depending on the manufacture of chemical substances specific to each plant, the characteristics of flower colour, leaf shape, form, size, smell, fruit, etc., are determined.

However, flower colour is perhaps the most sought-after aim of the breeder and new colour breaks do occur, and will do so again, spontaneously.

The dominant factors of both *F. magellanica* and *F. coccinea* proved the most influential of all the species in creating the classical form idealised by fuchsia enthusiasts and breeders. Although the red and mauve colour dominance was considered a handicap by the earlier hybridisers, later developments proved this to be an invalid concern and it is now known that flower colour can be modified almost at will by introducing white to the stronger colours. This is

131

reflected in the many pastel shades evident in todays cultivars.

Consequent to the earlier success in hybridising comes also the inherited ancestral polyploid constitution, bringing with it on the one hand breeding problems and on the other a variety of new strains of fuchsia hybrids carrying random polyploid conditions, many of which because of their large nuclei and therefore larger cells, produced size increases of plant, leaf, flower and fruit, a distinct advantage in many instances.

Studies into chromosome counts of the species fuchsia indicate that abnormalities had occurred in nature long before the species were collected, and such an occurrence can be found in the species *F. magellanica, F. coccinea* and *F. lycioides*. Each were to reveal a polyploid condition when examined and in all cases it would appear that the change was beneficial to their survival and an advantage over the diploid parental form.

A polyploid is an individual plant organism having chromosome compliments that deviate from the original diploid wild condition. Such organisms arise from abnormalities during chromosome duplication and separation into germ cells (gametes).

Examples of polyploidy found in modern fuchsia hybrids are of concern to all hybridists because although his choice of selection is very wide, there are many with odd sets of chromosomes, a condition in which either an extra chromosome is added or lost. These are known as heteroploids and as such are sterile because odd chromosomes cause a genetic imbalance.

The simple multiplication of chromosome numbers does not generate genetic imbalance and such plants are usually fertile with one another. These forms are known as autopolyploids and will be capable of crossing with other polyploids individuals. Such crosses in fact constitute the biggest bulk of today's hybrids.

Extensive cross breeding has produced many types of ploidy and examples to be found in modern hybrids extend from the original diploid type which has 2 sets of 11 chromosomes to:

| | |
|---|---|
| triploid | 3 sets of 11 chromosomes |
| tetraploid | 4 sets of 11 chromosomes |
| pentaploid | 5 sets of 11 chromosomes |
| hexaploid | 6 sets of 11 chromosomes |
| heptaploid | 7 sets of 11 chromosomes |
| octoploid | 8 sets of 11 chromosomes |

Sterile hybrids by some strange caprice of nature can occur as a result of crosses involving diploids and tetraploids, between tetraploids and hexaploids and, more remotely, between hexaploids and octoploids. Sterile triploid progeny are not uncommon in many

132

species and it is not unreasonable to suppose that the species *F. triphylla* is an example that colonised itself successfully in nature by vegetative propagation due in part to its superior vigour, gained by the abstinence from pollen and seed production.

In retrospect it is now not difficult to understand why little progress was made with the species *F. triphylla* when first introduced, and it must be obvious that the first hybrids were the result of chance chromosome doubling having occurred and the resultant restoration of fertility.

Crosses with *F. serratifolia, F. corymbiflora* and *F. fulgens*, would seem to be the most likely parents of the *triphylla* hybrids as we know them today, but it must be conceded that no spectacular new strains have developed from them over the years and we are still only distributing some dozen or more *triphylla* hybrids to the gardening public.

Some inherited incompatability seems to surround the species when attempting wide crosses, and it can only be conjectured that the genetic factors reject union. There appears to be no doubt that the specimen of *F. triphylla* held by botanical gardens is a triploid and is listed as such in the *Atlas of Chromosome Taxonomy*. Faced with this fact, one must ask how seed could be collected by Thomas Hogg in 1873 if indeed the plant was sterile, or again, what can be the true *F. triphylla* and does it exist as Father Plumier first discovered it around 1703?

Every hybridist will of course at some time meet the problem of sterility, frustrating an otherwise promising line of breeding. This to most amateurs is a disaster, as the means to overcome the barrier is for one reason or another not normally available to them, basically one supposes because the necessary drug is difficult to obtain.

The most effective means of treatment of plant cells to double the chromosome compliment is the drug colchicine and when used in the following concentration can be recommended as being an optimum which gives the highest rate of altered cells with a minimum of toxic reaction. 1 gram of colchicine dissolved in 500 ml water provides a relatively large quantity of the preparation for an amateur's needs, so if fine measure can be undertaken 0.1 gram to 50 ml water will be sufficient.

Keeping the drug in contact with the cells is usually achieved by dripping the solution onto cotton wool strips wrapped around the region of high active cellular division (the growing tip). The addition of agar to the aqueous solution to form a gel provides an easy method of application by brush, or alternatively the addition of glycerine will provide good adhesion.

Several strongly rooted cuttings of the selected plant are required, each to receive a different exposure time, varying from 12 to 96 hours.

It is important that high active growing conditions are maintained during exposure to the drug, if maximum effect is to be had. An ideal temperature to maintain would be 75 to 80°F.

Some exposures may have no effect, while others may be lethal. Favourable treatments on examination will reveal new leaves and stems, usually thicker and darker green with some slight crinkling and a coarser texture. Leaf profiles can differ by being more rounded and shorter and minute changes can be observed in veins and hairs if examined closely.

Experiments with seed can also be undertaken if so required by placing the germinating seed in solution. Different lots are removed after given intervals and in this way the most effective exposure can be determined by survival of treated seed.

Although an increase of flower size can in some instances be an added attraction the breeders greatest concern is to break any sterile barrier set up in a line of breeding, and it is the fervent hope that any reader able to pursue the procedure will not seek size purely for its own sake.

Luck plays a great part in any success you may have, but it is satisfying to know that the right ingredients have been used. The parents should collectively exhibit all the finer points or attributes one hopes to bring out.

More and more amateurs should be encouraged to take up this side of culture. The professionals are not very numerous in this country and most seem content to rely upon the amateurs for new introductions, so the field is wide open for anyone with vision. New colours may be limited, but varieties and form are endless.

# The Fuchsia Species

The genus *Fuchsia* is grouped into seven sections, totalling just over 100 distinct species and can be truly described as a plant of the Americas, because although a few arise in other places, such as Tahiti, New Zealand and the West Indies, nearly 95 per cent are native to South and Central America.

These are dispersed widely, covering a distance of almost 6,000 miles from northern Mexico through Guatemala, Honduras, El Salvador, Costa Rica, Panama, Colombia, Venezuela, Ecuador, Brazil, Bolivia, Peru, Chile and Argentina to the Magellan Strait, providing as diverse a range of form and habit of growth as they do natural habitat, with those from New Zealand seemingly far removed from the American species, showing an even greater diversity of characteristics between themselves.

Although few of the following species are in general cultivation in this country, there are nevertheless an appreciable amount grown in private collections and some experimental hybridisation is being carried out, though little is known of any success at the present time.

In 1943, Philip Munz, Professor of Botany at Pomona College, Claremont, California, produced as part of the Alice Eastwood Semi-Centennial Publications, a Revision of the genus *Fuchsia* (*Onagraceae*). This is still, some 35 years later, the most authoritative and detailed work accomplished over the entire range of species and varients of the *Fuchsia* genus, and reference to which has enabled this appendix to be far more enlightening than would otherwise have been possible.

## SECTION 1 *QUELUSIA*

*F. Campos-Portoi*  
*F. Bracelinae*  

*F. coccinea*  
*F. hybrida*

*F. magellanica*           *F. regia*

## SECTION 2 *EUFUCHSIA*

*F. splendens*

*F. cordifolia*

*F. austromontana*

*F. denticulata*

*F. leptopoda*

*F. Woytkowskii*

*F. magdalenae*

*F. canescens*

*F. rivularis*

*F. loxensis*

*F. pallescens*

*F. Townsendii*

*F. platypetala*

*F. macrostigma*

*F. ayavacensis*

*F. Pringsheimii*

*F. triphylla*

*F. petiolaris*

*F. Smithii*

*F. Asplundii*

*F. Llewelynii*

*F. venusta*

*F. Jahnii*

*F. Gehrigeri*

*F. simplicicaulis*

*F. confertifolia*

*F. Aspiazui*

*F. tincta*

*F. Mathewsii*

*F. Fischeri*

*F. Storkii*

*F. furfuracea*

*F. Munzii*

*F. hirtella*

*F. polyantha*

*F. corymbiflora*

*F. abrupta*

*F. Cuatrecasasii*

*F. Killipii*

*F. boliviana*

*F. fulgens*

*F. decussata*

*F. hypoleuca*

*F. scabriuscula*

*F. verrucosa*

*F. sanctae-rosae*

*F. Osgoodii*

*F. Andrei*

*F. Lehmannii*

*F. putumayensis*

*F. Hartwegii*

*F. ovalis*

*F. asperifolia*

*F. pilosa*

*F. glaberrima*

*F. macrophylla*

*F. sessilifolia*

*F. sylvatica*

## SECTION 3 *KIERSCHLEGERIA*

*F. lycioides*

## SECTION 4 *SKINNERA*

*F. excorticata*

*F. cyrtandroides*

*F. perscandens*

*F. procumbens*

*F. colensoi*                    *F. kirkii*


## SECTION 5 *HEMSLEYELLA*

*F. decidua*              *F. apetala*
*F. tuberosa*             *F. hirsuta*
*F. juntasensis*          *F. unduavensis*
*F. membranacea*         *F. Garleppiana*
*F. salicifolia*          *F. macrantha*
*F. tunariensis*          *F. cestroides*


## SECTION 6 *SCHUFIA*

*F. arborescens*


## SECTION 7 *ENCLIANDRA*

*F. thymifolia*           *F. microphylla*
*F. Pringlei*             *F. Hemsleyana*
*F. minimiflora*          *F. striolata*
*F. colimae*             *F. michoacanensis*
*F. tacanensis*           *F. Encliandra*
*F. Skutchiana*          *F. cylindracea*
*F. bacillaris*           *F. tetradactyla*
*F. minutiflora*          *F. Mexiae*


*F. Campos-Portoi* Pilger and Schulze 1935. Brazil. A native of Brazil,
which grows at an altitude of 7,000 ft in the region of Itatiaya, Serra
da Matiqueira, in the state of Rio de Janeiro.

A woody shrub, the branches of which separate widely, has a
narrow leaf with finely incurving serrations and is of a leathery texture. The small flower, tube and sepals, red with violet corolla, is
borne solitarily in upper leaf axils.

*F. Bracelinae* Munz 1943. Brazil. A woody, erect plant growing to a
height of 8-20 in with reddish, hairy stems. The leaf is ovate to lanceolate with a paler, reddish, hairy underside. A small flower of dark
red and purple colouring. This species is characterised by its herbaceous habit and tendency to throw off layers of basal bark. Dedicated by Munz to Mrs H.P. Bracelin of Berkeley, California.

*F. magellanica* Lammark 1788. Chile. A free branching shrub of bushy to semiscandent habit reaching a height of 5 ft or more and bearing red and purple flowers, at times in twos, in the upper leaf axils. This is the type species of a very large and variable family, many of which have been previously described in the hardy section. Used extensively by early hybridisers it has imparted a certain hardiness to many of our modern hybrids.

*F. coccinea* Soland 1789. Brazil? Slenderly branched bushy shrub which will grow to about 3 ft. A narrow, ovate leaf with paler underside, has some hair along main veins, leaves produced at times in threes. The flower is solitary in the upper axils and has a red tube and sepals with violet to purple corolla. Assessed by Munz to be probably of Brazilian origin, though when presented to Kew by Captain Firth was thought to have come from Chile.

*F. regia* Vand. Munz new comb. Brazil. *Quelusia regia*. Tall growing, up to about 18 ft freely branched shrub, younger growth very slender and dark red. Leaves are large, oblong-ovate, occurring at times in threes. Solitary-borne flowers have a deep red tube and sepals of a paler red, the corolla is purplish.

*F. splendens* Zuccarini 1832. Costa Rica. Sparsely branched, somewhat pendent shrub ranging from about 20 in to 8 ft in height and of tree-like proportions.

The ovate-cordate leaf has a paler underside and at times shows a red tinge. The interesting flower has a rose to bright red tube, green sepals with reddish base and green corolla; filaments of pale yellow terminate in yellow anthers, and the stigma is also green. A very distinctive species the native habitat of which ranges from Chiapas to Costa Rica at altitudes up to 10,000 ft.

*F. cordifolia* Bentham 1841. Guatemala. The mountains of Guatemala at elevations of between 8,000 to 11,000 ft are the natural habitat of this species. A straggling shrub from 3 ft in height up to that of a small tree, which at times is epiphytic. The thin, cordate to ovate leaf, has a paler underside and is often of reduced size in the area of the axils producing flowers which are borne solitary. The tube is a dull red, the sepals green with reddish outer base and the corolla is green to olive-green, anthers yellow.

*F. austromontana* Johnson 1939. Peru. Rather loose bushy shrub with red stems and light green leaf which has a paler underside where the veins exhibit a downy hair. Tube is light red with darker red sepals and red to purple corolla which often gives the flower an orangy hue, contrasting well with the leaf.

*F. denticulata* Ruiz and Pavon 1802. Peru and Bolivia. This is a semi-scandent shrub which will attain tree-like proportions up to a height of 35 ft. Elliptic to oblong fleshy leaf with light underside and very distinctive green upperside. The flower has a longish tube of red and red tipped green sepals, corolla crimson-scarlet, and white stigma and anthers.

The species has been used by the hybridist and crosses with Dominyana and *F. leptopoda* have been recorded, while quite recently Mr James Travis has produced a seedling using *F. denticulata* as the pollen parent. This seedling has a more dwarf and bushy habit with smaller leaves and flower, and the latter, although of similar colouring to the parent is very much brighter in all parts and might well become sought after by those who have previously grown its parent.

*F. leptopoda* Krause 1905. Peru. An erect though somewhat scandent shrub reaching a height of 7 ft. A light green oblanceolate leaf is the perfect foil to flowers which have a long, dark red tube, rather bulbous base, deep red sepals and fiery red corolla. Buds are long and pointed.

*F. Woytkowskii* Macbride 1941. Peru. Upright growing shrub with smooth, slender, purplish red younger growth and elliptic-lanceolate leaf, the upper surface of which is dark and smooth and paler underside. Flowering solitary in upper axils and toward the tips on shorter laterals. Tube of deep vermilion is nearly 2 in in length, sepals of vermilion give way to a corolla of bright red.

*F. magdalenae* Munz 1943. Colombia. A shrub with smooth purplish younger growth and leathery finely serrated dark veined elliptic leaf. Tube purplish at the base gradually changing to a brighter red as it merges with red sepals, corolla scarlet.

*F. canescens* Bentham 1845. Colombia. Freely branched, erect shrub reaching a height of some 6 or 7 ft with elliptic-ovate, finely serrated, leathery textured dark green leaf, with paler underside and downy hair on veins. The flowers which are axillary borne have slender pedicels, deep scarlet tube which is purple at bulbous base, divergent sepals deep scarlet, corolla scarlet, stigma scarlet. This species, although considered a native of Colombia, also reaches into Ecuador.

*F. rivularis* Macbride 1941. Peru. The ovate-elliptic leaf of the smooth upperside has a loose downy hair underneath and is somewhat reduced in size in upper parts where the flower is borne solitary in leaf axils. Very little is known of this species, although it is thought to be similar to *F. canescens* but with a larger leaf. Flower colouring: red tube and sepals with purplish corolla.

*F. loxensis* H.B.K. 1823. Ecuador. Slender, stiff and bushy shrub with purplish red slender stems which show yellowish hair. Deep green, shiny leaf has downy hair near to midrib and red main lateral veins on underside. Flowers are axillary borne and are solitary on slender pedicels. Tube deep red, sepals scarlet corolla red. Native habitat Loja at altitudes of between 6,000 and 11,000 ft.

*F. pallescens* Diels 1938. Ecuador. The mountain forest above Leito at an elevation of 9,000 ft is the natural home of this species which is a medium sized shrub with a pronounced toothed leaf. The axillary produced flowers are rather unusual with pale carmine tube, white sepals and purplish corolla.

*F. Townsendii* Johnson 1925. Ecuador. Densely spreading, downy haired shrub with purplish younger growth. The rather crowded leaves have widely spaced small teeth, are large, thin and hairy, the latter particularly on the underside. Flowers are axillary borne and sparse, having unusual tube shape, being very narrow for about one-third of their length, suddenly broadening toward sepals. Reddish-green tube, short red sepals with the corolla of short scarlet petals.

*F. platypetala* Johnson 1939. Peru. Shrub reaching nearly 10 ft in height with thin, finely serrated elliptic to lanceolate leaf on reddish, smooth and rounded stems. Tube red, long and thin, widening toward sepals which are crimson; corolla crimson with oblong white blotch through centre of each petal. An unusual species that would be welcomed into general cultivation.

*F. macrostigma* Bentham 1844. Ecuador. An openly branched erect shrub from 20 in to 5 ft high. Herbaceous type, younger growth has green to reddish colouring. The large, thin, dark green, finely serrated leaf has a lighter, purplish veined underside. Flowers solitary in upper leaf axils, with long cylindrical reddish purple tube, sepals somewhat paler, and corolla cerise to crimson. There are subspecies *F. macrostigma longiflora*, and *F. macrostigma typica* of which there is little information available.

*F. ayavacensis* Kris 1823. Peru and Ecuador. Branching, at times scandent shrub reaching to a height of nearly 10 ft with smooth, rounded, purplish younger growth. Thin, closely adjacent, finely serrated, purplish veined leaf, dark green with some hair on upperside, paler and downy haired on underside, flowering in upper axils.

Long, bulbous based, deep red tube. Reflexed spreading sepals and rounded crimson petals.

*F. Pringsheimii* Uban 1898. Santo Domingo. An openly branched shrub with purplish upper branches, growing to about 6 ft. The leaves, somewhat leathery textured on short jointed stems, are strongly bicoloured. Flowers produced in upper leaf axils. The long red tube is constricted for about half its length then widens toward red sepals. Corolla also red. This species differs from *F. triphylla* which flowers in an inflorescence and not in the leaf axils.

*F. triphylla* Plumier 1703. Santo Domingo. A semi-shrubby erect plant, growing from about 12-20 in high. Sparsely branched, younger growth reddish. Leaves of leathery texture, lance-ovate, becoming more crowded towards the top, bicoloured (copper-bronze) red veins. Upper leaves reducing to lance-ovate bracts where pendulous flowers are produced in dense terminal racemes. Red tube at first contracted, widening toward sepals of same colour, with petals of red, becoming lighter at base.

It is interesting to note that Munz describes that 'a collection from Massif de la Pelle, Marigot, near Jardins Bois-Pin, Haiti, Ekman H 1260 (US) has leaves of triphylla and flowers of Pringsheimii'.

*F. petiolaris* Kris 1823. Colombia. An erect shrub with reddish younger growth, reaching about 6 ft in height. Thin elliptic to ovate leaf is touched with purple. Flowers in uppermost axils giving impression of being racemose. Tube and sepals red, corolla deep red.

*F. Smithii* Munz 1943. Colombia. Woody vine growing to 6 ft, the drooping branches of which are reddish purple at the tips. This is another species with the habit of throwing off bark from the older wood. Leaf elliptic-ovate with lighter, downy-haired underside. Tube pinky-red to purplish red, sepals light to deep red, corolla dark to lighter red, with red stamens and cream anthers.

Natural habitat is rocky open hillsides in the vicinity of Vetas, at altitudes of about 10,000 ft.

*F. Asplundii* Macbride 1941. Peru. Free-branching, rather small shrub with red to orange longish flowers, which are produced singly in the axils of the main leaves. Upper leaves are somewhat reduced in size.

*F. Llewelynii* Macbride 1941. Peru. Shrub to about 3 ft bearing rather rigid leaves and narrow tubed flowers of red and violet, borne in slender racemes.

*F. venusta* Kris 1823. Colombia. A shrubby vine with dark red younger growth. Leaf elliptic and tending to leathery texture, rather short. Flowers in a pendant corymbose raceme at the end of branches. The flower has a red tube and sepals with carmine corolla which is held on long pedicels. Varieties of this species are, *F. venusta var. typica*, and *F. venusta var. huilensis.*

*F. Jahnii* Munz 1943. Venezuela. A scandent shrub, with young, slender, drooping and purplish growth. Elliptic, darkish green rather thin leaf. Sparsely flowered terminal corymbose racemes usual, but occasional axilary flowers. Thread-like pedicels to flowers which have tube and sepals red, and corolla light red with some hair on the back of petals, a condition that is similar with *F. venusta.*

*F. Gehrigeri* Gehriger 1930. Venezuela. Another rather scandent type shrub very often reaching about 15 ft, the reddish, slender, drooping branches accepting any support available. Evidence of some long, thin, soft hair in the region of the nodes, The leaf, finely serrated, is elliptic. Flowers dark red, in pendant terminal clusters and rather sparse.

*F. simplicicaulis* Ruiz and Pavon 1802. Peru. Slender stemmed shrub about 14 ft in height with tendency to grow up through other vegetation. Ends of branches are pendant. Leaves in whorls of four are linear-lanceolate and leathery textured. Flower long, bright red to purplish, produced in axils.

*F. confertifolia* Fielding and Gardner 1844. Peru. Profusely branched erect shrub growing to about 6 ft, the younger growths of which are covered with a dense, reddy-brown hair. The small leaf is oblong-ovate with a smooth upperside and some hair on the veins beneath. Flowers are sparse, pendant and subterminal. The tube is narrow near the base, abruptly widening for about two thirds of its total length, coloured dull red, with sepals a slightly lighter shade and corolla light red.

*F. Aspiazui* Macbride 1941. Peru. Sturdy shrub reaching a height of over 6 ft, the young growth of which is greenish. The large leaves are fleshy and yellowish green with pronounced veining. Many flowers are produced in a terminal pendant raceme. The tube, which is blood red, has a slightly bulbous base, gradually widening to divergent sepals and a corolla of scarlet.

*F. tincta* Johnson 1939. Peru. The young growth of this shrub is of a brownish-red hue with evidence of some fine brown hair. Thin leaves are generally elliptic to ovate with serrations along the edges. Both leaf surfaces show a purplish hue and some very fine hair, particularly on the underside. The flower, which is nearly 1½ in long, has a deep crimson tube which is narrowed toward the base, gradually widening to divergent crimson sepals and a scarlet-crimson corolla. Flowers are borne in terminal racemes on a shrub that will achieve a height of 5 ft.

*F. Mathewsii* Macbride 1941. Peru. On this species the branches and underside of leaves are covered with a reddy-brown, fine, but dense hair. The leaf is broad, elliptic and a little over 3 in long.

There is very little information available on this species although it is said to be very similar to *F. pilosa* but with a larger flower.

*F. Fischeri* Macbride 1941. Peru. Of a rather lax habit, the younger growth is of reddish colouring and the leaf is oblong-lanceolate with prominent veins on the underside, both surfaces being covered with a dense soft hair. Flowers have a pinkish tube and sepals and purple corolla. This is another species of which there are few details available though it is thought to be near *F. Mathewsii* but with a less broad leaf.

*F. Storkii* Munz 1943. Peru. An erect shrub growing to about 10 ft in height; younger growths are reddish with some fine hair of similar colouring. Leaves generally elliptic to oblanceolate, slightly serrated with light green upper surface and somewhat paler underside. Flowers are sparse and produced terminally, having a dark red tube, with sepals and corolla deep red.

*F. furfuracea* Johnson 1925. Bolivia. The leaves of this rather spreading shrubby species have both surfaces covered with a fine brown hair. A limited quantity of flowers, with long pedicels, are borne in terminal racemes; the tube and sepals are red, corolla purplish-red.

*F. Munzii* Macbride 1941. Peru. A rather sparsely flowered species with almost red self flowers which are borne in panicles at the end of the branches. Unfortunately few details are available. Named in honour of Philip Munz.

*F. hirtella* Kris 1823. Colombia. From the mountains near Fusagasuga, Cundimaria, this is a species with the somewhat unusual habit of exfoliating older branches. The young growth is reddish in colour and the leaves are dark green on upper surfaces with a paler underside. Flowers are grouped in panicles on short slender pedicels with tubes rose red, sepals and corolla red.

*F. polyantha* Killip 1935. Colombia. A species of bushy habit growing to about 3 ft, it has purplish red stems and rather rigid, light green leaves. The tube is purplish-red, sepals scarlet, corolla crimson. Flowers are many and produced in pendulous panicles.

*F. corymbiflora* Ruiz and Pavon. Ecuador. A sparsely branched rather scandent shrub reaching to about 16 ft. The leaves are broadly oblong-lanceolate with inconspicuous small teeth. Flowers terminally clustered. Long scarlet tube, narrow, widening gradually to erect, divergent scarlet sepals and deep red corolla.

*F. abrupta* Johnson 1925. Peru. Scandent shrub with smooth widely separating branches and leaves tending to leathery texture, dark green. Flowering is in terminal pendant racemes on long pedicels. Tube and sepals scarlet, as is the corolla.

*F. Cuatrecasasii* Cuatrecasas 1940. Colombia. Shrub with smooth green younger growth. The thin elliptic-ovate leaf is smooth and light green. Flowers sparse, produced in short terminal racemes on slender pedicels, tube bright red, narrow for about one third of the total length gradually widening to divergent scarlet sepals and scarlet corolla. Grows in its natural habitat at altitudes from 5,000-7,000 ft.

*F. Killipii* Johnson 1928. Colombia. A scandent shrub reaching some 13 ft, the young growth smooth and of a brownish hue. An elliptic leaf of leathery texture. Quite heavily flowered from upper axils and in drooping terminal racemes. The tube is narrowed from near the base for one-third its total length then abruptly widens to the base of the sepals. Tube and sepals red, corolla bright red.

*F. boliviana* Carr 1876. Bolivia. Open branching bushy shrub, almost reaching 18 ft in height in its native habitat. Young growth is covered with a thick longish hair. Leaves are generally elliptic with fine serrations. The flower is produced in lax terminal panicles. Tube and spreading sepals dark red, corolla a lighter shade of red. Varieties of *F. boliviana* include; *F. boliviana var. typica, F. boliviana var. puberulenta*, and *F. boliviana var. luxurians*.

*F. fulgens* De Candolle 1828. Mexico. Varying from 1-4 ft in height this shrub, possibly epiphyte, has tuberous roots and soft woody stems, the latter together with the leaves being tinged slightly red. The broad thinnish leaf is sage-green and very hairy. A long tube is dull scarlet which gradually widens toward yellowish-green sepals that have a yellow, at times red, base; corolla bright red, style pink, stigma greenish. In its natural habitat it probably grows on walls and ledges. Flowers are produced in large terminal clusters. The recorded natural varients of this species are: *F. fulgens carminata, F. fulgens gesneriana, F. fulgens rubra grandiflora,* and *F. fulgens multiflora pumila,* but there seems little doubt that there are other plants in cultivation that do not come into this category, but do look very similar. *F. fulgens* is a very popular species and is often seen on the show bench, where it always attracts attention.

*F. deccusata* Ruiz and Pavon 1802. Peru. A shrub which relies on other vegetation for support, eventually attaining a height of 10 ft. Characterised by its long wandering branches, the younger growth of which is red in colour and covered with a thick brown incurving hair. The leaves are many, elliptic-lanceolate, dark green, finely serrated and of a leathery texture. Tube red, widely separated sepals are red tipped green, corolla red. Another species that is occasionally seen on the show bench.

*F. hypoleuca* Johnson 1925. Ecuador. Slender stemmed shrub about 5 ft in height with very crowded lanceolate and rigid leaves, the undersides of which are covered with a dense, fine hair, which at times it would seem becomes the home of fungus mycelia. Tube red; widely separated sepals and corolla are scarlet. Flower pendulous and solitary in leaf axils.

*F. scabriuscula* Bentham 1845. Ecuador. Of low spreading habit, between 20 in and 5 ft high, the young growth is of reddish colouring and covered with a dense white to brownish hair. The elliptic-obovate leaf is rigid and pronouncedly veined. The flower is of bright red, with tube, sepals and corolla of a slightly darker shade. Slender pedicels hold the flowers singly in leaf axils.

*F. verrucosa* Hartweg 1845. Colombia. An erect shrub between 3-6 ft in height, has a thick firm leaf which is slightly serrated. A sparsely flowered species with the flower borne solitary in leaf axils. Tube and sepals bright red; corolla slightly darker red.

*F. sanctae-rosae* Kuntze 1898. Bolivia. A very variable and contradictory growth habit from herbaceous and 12 in high to shrubby and heights of between 6-9 ft, erect to semidecumbent. Most young growths are of a purplish-red colouring and smooth, but others at times show a fine hair. An elliptic-lanceolate leaf smooth and deep green on upperside, lighter beneath. The many flowers are solitary

145

in upper leaf axils on very slender pedicels. Tube bright red, sepals scarlet, corolla orange-red to scarlet, stigma red. Natural habitat ranges from southern Peru into Bolivia at altitudes between 7,000 and 10,000 ft.

*F. Osgoodii* Macbride 1941. Peru. An erect shrub reaching to 12 ft in height, with deep green, firm, elliptic-lanceolate leaf. Flowers are few and produced in bunched racemes. Tube dark red and about 1 in long, sepals and corolla red.

*F. Andrei* Johnson 1925. Ecuador. Low-growing shrub, young growth purplish-red. Leaves are thin and generally oblong-elliptic. The flower is mostly in terminal racemes on slender pedicels. Tube slightly over 1 in long, greenish-red with purplish-red corolla.

*F. Lehmanii* Munz 1943. Ecuador. A soft-wooded shrub of some 6 ft in height. Young growths are dark red and smooth, with rigid leaves of dark green on the upperside, paler and red veined with some sign of hair beneath. Many flowers in short and crowded terminal and lateral racemes. Dark red tube with reflexed spreading scarlet sepals; corolla scarlet.

*F. putumayensis* Munz 1943. Colombia. Shrub with thinnish, lance-ovate leaves of bright green with prominently veined underside. Flowers in short compact terminal and lateral racemes. Tube bright red; divergent sepals and corolla scarlet.

*F. Hartwegii* Bentham 1945. Colombia. Slenderly branched erect shrub with thin leaf of dark green. Many flowers in terminal pendulous panicles on slender pedicels. Tube red, sepals orange-red to scarlet, corolla red.

*F. ovalis* Ruiz and Pavon 1802. Peru. Erect and semishrubby, sparsely branched to about 3 ft with large thin leaf of darkish green. Tube and sepals scarlet, corolla purplish-scarlet, filaments violet. Flowers borne in axillary racemes.

*F. asperifolia* Krause 1905. Peru. Low-growing shrub about 18 in high, somewhat sparsely branched, young growth covered with fine hair, leaves thin and hairy. Tube and sepals dark red, corolla scarlet. Flowers held on very short pedicels in terminal racemes.

*F. pilosa* Fielding and Gardener 1941. Peru. This shrub, as its name suggests, is practically covered with fine, white hair, particularly on the branches, leaves and tubes. The oblong-lanceolate leaf has very small serrations. One leaf in each whorl of three is slightly larger than the other two, and another oddity appears in the petioles, two of which are of equal length, with the third over twice as long. Flowering is in terminal racemes. Flower is a scarlet self, about 1 in long.

*F. glaberrima* Johnson 1925. Ecuador. An upright shrub, young growth reddish. Leaf firm, tinged reddish-purple. Flowering in short terminal racemes, the tube is bright red, slightly contracted at the base, gradually widening to scarlet sepals; corolla scarlet.

*F. macrophylla* Johnson 1925. Peru. Shrub up to 6 ft in height; young growth with dark red to purplish tinge; leaves elliptic, dark green. Tube scarlet; sepals divergent, red with green tips; corolla bright red. Flowering is usually axillary but at times in terminal racemes.

*F. sessilifolia* Bentham 1845. Ecuador. A slender and erect shrub reaching dimensions of a small tree, with young growths of purplish-red. Leaves firm, generally elliptic-lanceolate, leathery textured and glossy green with a paler underside. Flowering is terminal and lax. Tube scarlet, sepals greenish-red, corolla scarlet. Native to southern Colombia and northern Ecuador at altitudes ranging from 6,000 to nearly 10,000 ft.

*F. sylvatica* Bentham 1845. Ecuador. Low-growing shrub somewhat scandent, openly branched. Leaf elliptic-ovate, thin, deep green on upper surface with a paler underside where the veins are reddish. Flowering is in lateral or terminal pendant racemes. Tube pinky-red, sepals pink, corolla crimson to purple-red.

*F. lycioides* Andrews 1807. Chile. Stout upright shrub reaching 9 ft in height, with older wood of a greyish colour. The many leaves are lance-ovate. Tube and sepals red, corolla purple. Flowers are axillary and singly borne, pedicels thread-like giving pendulous effect to flowers. This species is obtainable in this country, possibly due in part to the fact that it is hardy.

*F. excorticata* Forster 1776. New Zealand. A very wide spreading tree reaching heights of 30 ft in its natural habitat. This is another species that exfoliates a parchment-like bark. Leaves lance-ovate, with a green upper surface and white underside. Flowers solitary, pendant and axillary. Tube and sepals initially green changing to purplish-red, corolla dark purple, anthers blue, stigma yellowish.

*F. cyrtandroides* Moore 1940. Tahiti. A lone species from these islands, its natural habitat is the rain forests at an altitude of some 5,000 ft where it grows to tree-like proportions of 15 ft in height. Leaves broad elliptic, with a green upper surface, white beneath. Rose-magenta flowers are axillary and produced singly in leaf axils.

*F. colensoi* Hook 1867. New Zealand. A small erect branching shrub. Leaves have a green upper surface and a white underside. Tube red, sepals greeny-red, corolla purple.

*F. perscandens* Cockayne and Allen 1927. New Zealand. A climbing shrub from the forests near Fielding, North Island. Flower said to be similar to *F. Colensoi*. Leaf has a whitish underside.

*F. procumbens* Cunningham 1893. New Zealand. Another species from North Island, in the vicinity of the village of Matauri. This is probably the most popular and widely grown of all the fuchsia species and is always to be seen on the show bench.

It is a procumbent woody plant with slender stems on which the leaves are situated alternately. The leaves are round to ovate with fine serrations. Flowers are held upright, and are solitary and axillary on slender pedicels. An unusual and interesting flower of dull yellow tube and greenish reflexed sepals, petals are absent. The fruit is large and pinky-red, and its presence is always acceptable in show plants.

*F. kirkii* Hooker 1871. New Zealand. From the Great Barrier Island, this is also of prostrate habit, with slender stems and upward pointing flowers, similar in many ways to *F. procumbens*, though not in flower colour. Tube dull red shading to greenish-yellow, sepals green with purple tips.

*F. decidua* Standley 1929. Mexico. So named because the shrub is deciduous at the time of flowering. Flowers are borne on slender pedicels in short racemose lateral panicles. Tube light vermilion, sepals vermilion, corolla of insignificant almost minute petals about 2 mm long.

*F. tuberosa* Krause 1905. Peru. An epiphytic shrub reaching 3 ft in height, with roots that bear clusters of tubers. Stems sparsely branched and of a reddish colouring. Leaves are lanceolate and somewhat toothed, probably exfoliated at flowering period. Flowers produced in upper axils on slender pedicels. Tube red, narrowed from near base, widening suddenly toward erect, divergent green sepals; petals absent, stamens yellow.

*F. juntasensis* Kuntze 1898. Bolivia. A vine-like epiphytic shrub, sparsely branched, about 20 in in height, with purplish younger growth. Older wood tends to lose outer bark. The few flowers, usually crowded, are produced in terminal racemose clusters. Tube rose to flesh coloured, sepals red, petals absent, anthers cream, stigma green.

*F. membranacea* Hemsley 1876. Venezuela. Rather thin-leafed shrub with greenish-red flower which is borne axillary.

*F. salicifolia* Hemsley 1876. Bolivia. Sparsely branched epiphytic shrub, the younger growth of which is purplish. A rather thickish leaf, and flower of yellowish green, lacking petals.

*F. tunariensis* Kuntze 1898. Bolivia. A tuberous rooted epiphytic or prostrate to scandent shrub, with stems about 20 in long. An oblong-ovate leaf, somewhat thin. Flowers sparse, produced singly in uppermost axils. Tube is a reddy-pink, sepals red, petals absent.

*F. apetala* Ruiz and Pavon 1802. Peru. A vine-like shrub to about 3 ft, usually relying on other vegetation for support, with reddish younger growth. An elliptic-ovate leaf, somewhat leathery textured, with a hairy underside. Sparsely flowered from tops of branches. Tube orange-scarlet and rather bulbous based; spreading orange to red sepals, petals absent, anthers green. Native also to Venezuela and Ecuador.

*F. hirsuta* Hemsley 1876. Peru. A climbing epiphytic shrub, sparsely branched and tuberous rooted. Young growths are stout and knotty, covered with a dense fine white hair. Thinnish leaf with some serrations, oblong-ovate, densely hairy when young. The ovaries also exhibit a shaggy hair. Flowers on slender pedicels are usually grouped near the tips, particularly on lateral branches. Tube fiery-purplish-red and covered with a dense fine hair; sepals red, the backs of which also have a covering of fine hair; petals absent. This species usually exfoliates at the time of flowering. (Also arising in Brazil.)

*F. unduavensis* Munz 1943. Bolivia. This species is said to be very much like *F. hirsuta*, the main difference being that it is in full leaf during the flowering period. The younger growths, ovaries, pedicels and tubes are covered with a fine brown hair.

*F. Garleppiana* Kuntze and Wittmack 1893. Bolivia. A slender stemmed, sparsely branched species with tuberous roots. Reaches about 3 ft in height, at times epiphytic. Leaf is generally oblong-ovate and rather thin. Flowering in the axils of the main branches on slender pedicels. Tube and sepals pink, petals absent. Another species exhibiting hair on the sepals, in this case, on both sides.

*F. macrantha* Hooker 1846. Peru. A low trailing sparsely branched epiphytic shrub, with an elliptic-ovate leaf which is lost at the time of flowering. Flowers have slender pedicels, and are produced on the younger lateral growths. Tube and sepals coral, sepals tipped light green, petals absent, stigma green.

*F. cestroides* Schulze and Menz 1940. Mexico and Panama. An erect shrub 3 ft in height with young growth of reddish colouring. Oblong-ovate leaf, finely serrated with fine hair beneath. Profusely flowered in terminal panicles. Tube dark red, narrow near base gradually widening toward dark red sepals.

*F. arrborescens* Sims 1826. Mexico and Panama. A low-growing shrub, at times epiphytic, which can also take on the characteristics of a small tree when it may reach heights of 25 ft. An oblong-ovate leaf has a lighter underside with the veins tinged red. The flowers are profuse in corymbose panicles. Tube rose magenta, sepals reddish-purple, corolla lilac, filaments pinky-lavender with purple anthers, stigma purple. Mr James Travis has recently had some success using this species in hybridisation.

*F. thymifolia* Kris 1823. Mexico. An openly branched shrub reaching about 3 ft in height, with slender, reddish young growth. Leaf elliptic-ovate, somewhat thin, with paler underside. Flowers pinky-white, darkening with age, borne solitary in leaf axils.

*F. Pringlei* Robinson and Seaton 1893. Mexico. Very similar to *F. thymifolia* but with leaves closer together. Flowers small, pale pink.

*F. minimiflora* Hemsley 1880. Mexico. A loosely-branched shrub from 3-12 ft in height, rather slender growth with elliptic-ovate leaves. Flowers are borne solitary in axils and are white flushed red, minute, the smallest flower of the whole species. Sepals are reflexed and spreading. A delightful species, often seen on the show bench.

*F. colimae* Munz 1943. Mexico. A habit very similar to *F. minimiflora*. Tube whitish-green, reflexed spreading white sepals, corolla white.

*F. tacanensis* Lundell 1940. Mexico. Reaching heights of 12 ft in its natural habitat this is an openly-branched species with large thin, toothed leaves. Tube green, sepals greeny-white, corolla pinky-white tending to reddish in the older flowers.

*F. Skutchiana* Munz 1943. Guatemala. An erect shrub similar in habit to *F. tacanensis*. Small flower pinky-white, ageing to red.

*F. bacillaris* Lindley 1832. Guatemala. A shrub between 3-6 ft in height, openly branched. Finely serrated, somewhat leathery textured, generally elliptic-ovate leaf. Tube red, sepals and corolla rose.

*F. minutiflora* Hemsley 1878. Trinidad and Mexico. At times reaching nearly 6 ft in height this is a slenderly branched species with rather thickish leaves which are widely toothed. Tube and sepals red; corolla white. Flowers are solitary in leaf axils.

*F. microphylla* Kris 1823. Mexico. A shortish, many-branched shrub to about 3 ft. Dark green, leathery textured leaf, rather crowded and sharply serrated, with a lighter underside. Flower small, tube and sepals dark red, corolla rose. Another of the Breviflorae section which is often seen on the show bench.

*F. Hemsleyana* Woodson and Seibert 1937. Costa Rica and Panama. Will reach heights of between 3-9 ft in its mountainous habitat. The terminal branches are very slender; the leaf is small, leathery textured, somewhat serrated and closely adjacent. The flowers are borne solitary in leaf axils, on thread-like pedicels. The tiny flower of rose colouring has a tinge of purple in the petals.

*F. striolata* Lundell 1940. Mexico. A rather scandent openly branched shrub with a lance-ovate, thickish to leathery, leaf. A small red flower is borne solitary on short pedicels.

*F. michoacanensis* Sesse and Mocino 1887-90. Costa Rica. A species ranging from Mexico to Costa Rica. This species will reach heights of 9 ft, slenderly branched with fine hair on younger growths. An elliptic-ovate, rather thin leaf which has a hairy underside. Flowers are axillary borne with tube and sepals red, corolla coral-red. Occasionally seen on the show bench.

*F. Encliandra* Steudel 1840. Mexico. A thickly branched shrub reaching heights of up to 12 ft, with a small lance-ovate leaf which is rather thin. The very tiny flower is borne solitary in leaf axils on thread-like pedicels. This is the type species of the *Encliandra* (*Breviflorae*) section.

*F. cylindracea* Lindley 1838. Mexico. In its natural habitat this species will attain heights of 15 ft. It is fairly erect though somewhat openly branched, the tips of the younger growths of a purplish colouring with some signs of a coarse hair. Leaves obovate to elliptic, rather thin. Flowers are borne solitary in the leaf axils. Male and female flowers are borne on separate plants. Tube cylindrical, dark red; sepals red, corolla red.

*F. tetradactyla* Lindley 1846. Guatemala. An openly branched shrub to about 8 ft in height, ends of younger growth of reddish colouring. Leaves are broad, ovate, rather thin with some signs of serrations, a fine hair on upper and lower surfaces. Flowers on thread-like pedicels are borne singly in the leaf axils. Male and female flowers borne on separate plants. Tube rose-orchid to deep red, sepals red to orchid, corolla pale rose-scarlet. Female flowers somewhat smaller.

*F. Mexiae* Munz 1943. Mexico. Large leafy shrub. The younger, slender growths are reddish. Leaves thin with some serration. Flowers axillary, with male and female flowers produced on separate plants. Female flower has a tube barely 1 mm wide and ovate sepals which are red, petals white. Natural habitat is the dry pine forest at elevations of some 5,000 ft.

*F. Vargasiana* Munz. C.V. Calderson 1973 (Isotype). Found between Yanamaygo and Rio Tambomayo at an elevation of over 7,000 ft in July 1936 in the forest of the lower 'Ceja'. Has often been confused in the past with *F. tincta* to which it is very close, but it differs from this in the size of the perianth, as well as other differentiating characters. A shrub which attains a height of some 5 ft.

The above information is from a translation by Dr Paul Parker of Leicester University, of *Ecological and Taxonomic Notes* by Professor C.V. Calderson of the University of Cuzco.

# Directory of Specialist Fuchsia Societies

The following is a list of specialist fuchsia societies. These are without exception affiliated to the BFS and have the same objectives, i.e., 'to encourage, improve and extend the cultivation of Fuchsias in all possible ways, to research, collect and disseminate information to that end, to hold shows and exhibitions of Fuchsias and to co-operate with other Societies pursuing the same objects'.

For the beginner, membership of one of the societies listed will entitle him or her to monthly lectures, film shows, practical demonstrations, participation in the society's competitions and shows, etc. All are highly recommended and very good value for a modest annual subscription.

Barnet & District Fuchsia Society
Miss J. Muller, Hon. Secretary
2 Norman Court
Potters Bar
Hertfordshire

Birmingham & District Fuchsia Society
Mrs J. Morris, Hon. Secretary
53 Cherry Orchard Road
Handsworth Wood
Birmingham B20 2LD

Border Counties Carnation & Fuchsia Society
Mr L. Twigg, Hon. Secretary
Dykeside Cottage
Longtown
Carlisle
Cumbria

Cambridge & District Fuchsia Society
Mr C. W. Napthen, Hon. Secretary
41 Bishops Road
Trumpington
Cambridge

Central Scotland Fuchsia Group
Mr J. Waugh, Hon. Secretary
The Mains House
Inverleith Park
Edinburgh EH3 5N7

Cissbury Fuchsia & Pelargonium Society
Mr L. Hobbs, Hon. Secretary
39 Downside Avenue
Findon Valley
Worthing
West Sussex BN14 OEU

Colchester & District Fuchsia Society
Mrs P. Brown, Hon. Secretary
Pilgrims
Stanway Green
Colchester
Essex

Cotswold Fuchsia & Pelargonium Society
Mr A. I. Peacock, Hon. Secretary
10 Hollis Gardens
Up Hatherley
Cheltenham
Gloucester GL51 6JQ

Derby & District Fuchsia Society
Mr R. H. Gregson, Hon. Secretary
41 Willson Road
Littleover
Derby

Devon & Cornwall Fuchsia & Geranium Society
Mrs V. K. Ellan, Hon. Secretary
22 Barne Road
St Budeaux
Plymouth PL5 1EF

Dorking & District Fuchsia Society
Mrs L. A. Wright, Hon. Secretary
91 Parks Way
Dorking
Surrey RH4 1ET

Dukeries Fuchsia, Pelargonium and Pot Plant Group
Mrs P. Cook, Hon. Secretary
34 Sherwood
Worksop
Notts S80

East Anglian Fuchsia Fellowship
Mr E. J. Goulding, Hon. Secretary
44 Lonsdale Close
Ipswich
Suffolk

East Kent Fuchsia Society
Mrs H. Bethel, Hon. Secretary
99 Cherry Drive
Canterbury
Kent

Edenbridge Fuchsia & Pelargonium Society
Mr R. Holmes, Hon. Secretary
4 Pine Grove
Edenbridge
Kent TN8 5HU

Elmbridge Fuchsia & Pelargonium Society
Mr A. A. Mills, Hon. Secretary
1 Campbell Road
Weybridge
Surrey

Enfield & District Fuchsia Society
Mr W. J. Sherman, Hon. Secretary
47 Hillcrest
Winchmore Hill
London N21 1AT

Epping & District Fuchsia Society
Mr D. J. Wilding, Hon. Secretary
1 Wintry Park Cottages
Thornwood Road
Epping
Essex

Guildford Fuchsia Group
Mrs J. A. Tutt, Hon. Secretary
22 Dawnay Road
Great Bookham
Leatherhead
Surrey

Harrow Fuchsia Society
Mr A. K. Blackburn, Hon. Secretary
25 Park View
Hatch End
Pinner, Middlesex

Horley Gardeners Assoc. Fuchsia & Pelargonium Group
Mrs F. Denton, Hon. Secretary
Verona
Horley Road
Charlwood
Horley
Surrey

Knaresborough & District Fuchsia & Pelargonium Society
Mr A. H. Latty, Hon. Secretary
10 Plompton Grove
Harrogate HG2 7DP

Leicestershire Fuchsia Society
Mr R. J. White, Hon. Secretary
79 Liberty Road
Glenfield
Leicester

Manchester & District Fuchsia Group
Mr N. Hobbs, Hon. Secretary
19 Altrincham Road
Gatley
Cheadle
Cheshire SK8 4EL

Merseyside Fuchsia Group
Mr J. Berry, Hon. Secretary
34 Templemore Road
Oxton
Birkenhead
Merseyside L43 2HB

Metropolitan Essex Fuchsia Society
Mr W. Middlebrook, Hon. Secretary
150 Empress Avenue
Ilford,
Essex, IG1 3DF

Mid Kent Fuchsia Group
Mrs C. Keyes, Hon. Secretary
Peacehaven
21 Buckland Lane
London Road
Maidstone
Kent ME16 OBJ

Mid Wessex Fuchsia & Pelargonium Society
Mr W. S. Coleman, Hon. Secretary
86 Carfax Avenue
Tongham
Nr. Farnham
Surrey

New Forest & District Fuchsia Society
Mr R. H. Dart, Hon. Secretary
37a Jacobs Gutter
Hounsdown
Totton
Hants SO4 4FQ

Northampton & District Fuchsia Society
Mr R. N. Edmondson, Hon. Secretary
85 Green Street
Milton Malsar
Northampton NN7 3AT

North Devon Fuchsia Society
Mrs F. Avery, Hon. Secretary
Little Orchard
Chixcombe Lane
Northam
North Devon

North West Kent Fuchsia & Pelargonium Society
Mr R. A. Borkett, Hon. Secretary
8 Fernheathway
Wilmington
Dartford
Kent

North Worcestershire Fuchsia Society
Mrs V. Ridding, Hon. Secretary
Fuchsia Vale Nurseries
Stanklyn Lane
Summerfield
Kidderminster
Worcestershire D710 4HS

Norwich & District Fuchsia & Pelargonium Society
Mr R. Clitheroe, Hon. Secretary
37 Firs Road
Hellesdon
Norwich NR6 6UB

Nottingham & Notts Fuchsia Society
Mr G. Thorley, Hon. Secretary
60 Co-operative Avenue
Hucknall
Nottingham NG15 7AJ

Nuneaton Rose, Fuchsia & Sweet Pea Society
Mr K. T. Payne, Hon. Secretary
160 Croft Road
Stockingford
Nuneaton
Warwickshire CV10 7OW

Reading & District Fuchsia Society
Mr G. E. Bartlett, Hon. Secretary
11 Hungerford Drive
Reading
Berks

Reigate & District Fuchsia Society
Mrs Boniface, Hon. Secretary
10 Surrey Hills
Boxhill Road
Tadworth
Surrey

Rotherham & District Fuchsia Group
Mr J. T. Warner, Hon. Secretary
35 Foster Road
Wickersley
Rotherham
South Yorks S66 OHJ

Sheffield Fuchsia & Greenhouse Society
Mrs M. Knowles, Hon. Secretary
171 Woodseats Road
Sheffield
Yorkshire S80 PL

Solent Fuchsia Club
Mrs E. Stevens, Hon. Secretary
7 Gaylyn Way
Fareham
Hants

South Devon Fuchsia Society
Mrs S. Driver, Hon. Secretary
90 Primley Park
Paignton
South Devon TQ3 3JX

South East Essex Fuchsia Fellowship
Mrs J. Wood, Hon. Secretary
19 Eastern Road
Rayleigh
Essex

South Lakeland Fuchsia Society
Mr J. Mull, Hon. Secretary
37 Wattsfield Road
Kendal
Cumbria

South Wales Fuchsia Group
Mrs A. Searle, Hon. Secretary
5 Milford Close
Ton Teg
Nr. Pontypridd
Glamorgan

Spa Hill & District Fuchsia Group
Mr W. Tann, Hon. Secretary
89 Moffat Road
Thornton Heath
Surrey CR4 8PY

Squirrels Heath & District Horticultural Society
Mrs K. Crampton, Hon. Secretary
15 Cranbrook Drive
Gidea Park
Romford
Essex

Sussex Wagtails Fuchsia Club
Mr G. N. Woodhams, Hon. Secretary
8 Fernhurst Close
Ifield
Crawley
Sussex RH11 OAW

Sutton Coldfield Fuchsia Society
Mr J. L. Kirby, Hon. Secretary
68 Nicholas Road
Sutton Coldfield
West Midlands B74 3QS

Tees & Wear Fuchsia & Pelargonium Society
Mr H. Johnson, Hon. Secretary
24 Cumrie Road
Hartlepool
Cleveland CS25 3AJ

Teeside Fuchsia & Begonia Society
Mr S. Denney, Hon. Secretary
1 Trigo Close
Marton Manor Park
Middlesborough TS7 8RS

Thames Valley Fuchsia & Pelargonium Society
Mr W. Ings, Hon. Secretary
96 Queens Walk
South Ruislip
Middlesex HA4 ONS

Thanet Fuchsia Group
Mr E. Paice, Hon. Secretary
3 Beacon Road
St. Peters
Broadstairs
Kent

The Geranium & Fuchsia Society of Mid & West Cornwall
Mr J. F. Lanigan, Hon. Secretary
Castle View
Trerarwah Lane
Rosevogeon
Penzance
Cornwall

The Midland Geranium, Glasshouse & Garden Society
Miss S. Baynham, Hon. Secretary
179 Poplar Avenue
Birmingham 17

Three Counties Fuchsia Society
Mr B. Turvey, Hon. Secretary
217 Bristol Road
Gloucester

Timperley & District Chrysanthemum & Fuchsia Society
Mr K. Ward, Hon. Secretary
5 Pollen Close
Sale
Cheshire M33 3LP

Waverley Fuchsia Group
Mrs M. Sutton, Hon. Secretary
Orchard House
Tilthems Corner
Godalming
Surrey

Wessex Fuchsia Group
Mrs R. Witts, Hon. Secretary
170 Ladyfield Road
Chippenham
Wilts SN14 OAP

West Yorkshire Fuchsia Society
Mr E. A. Johns, Hon. Secretary
85 Larkfield Road
Harrogate
North Yorks

Wrexham & District Fuchsia & Geranium Society
Mrs G. O. Whittle, Hon. Secretary
57 Saxon Street
Wrexham
Clwyd LL13 7BB

The British Fuchsia Society
Mr R. Ewart, Hon. Secretary
The Bungalow
Brookwood Military Cemetery
Brookwood
Surrey

Fuchsia
Societies
Overseas

American Fuchsia Society
Hall of Flowers
Golden Gate Park
San Francisco
California 94122
USA

National Fuchsia Society
Mrs Ida Drapkin, Hon. Secretary
6121 Monero Drive
Rancho Palos Verdes
California 90274
USA

# Glossary of Terms

*Aerosol*: a pressurised metal container designed to release an atomised insecticidal vapour.

*Anther*: the pollen-bearing part of a stamen.

*Back cross*: F1 generation crossed back to either parent, producing a second reciprocal generation (R 2).

*Bud*: undeveloped shoot bearing overlapping leaves; also a term used for flower initial.

*Calyx*: the outermost group of floral parts (sepals).

*Chromosome*: thread-like bodies consisting of a series of different genes arranged in linear fashion. Occurring in the nucleus of every plant cell.

*Corolla*: the internal envelope or floral leaves of a flower.

*Cross bred*: a plant or group of plants produced by hybridisation.

*Cultivar*: the internationally accepted term for what is commonly known as a 'cultivated variety' or simply a 'variety'.

*Fertilisation*: union of male and female cells.

*Filament*: stem of an anther.

*F1*: first filial generation. Offspring resulting from parental cross.

*F2*: second filial generation. Offspring resulting from the crossing of F1 siblings among themselves.

*Gene*: heredity factor. One unit of a chromosome, influencing a particular character or characters in a particular way.

*Growing tip*: (apical mersitem). Providing for growth in length of stem. Also site of leaf and buds.

*Hybrid*: offspring derived from the crossing of two distinct species.

*Lateral growth*: side growth of branches, sometimes called breaks.

*Leaf axil*: the connection between leaf stalk and stem.

*Leaf Node*: swelling of the stem to which the leaf is attached.

*Mutation*: (sport). Sudden departure from parent type.

*Ovary*: the enlarged lower part of the pistil enclosing the ovules.

*Photosynthesis*: synthesis of organic compounds from water and carbon dioxide, using energy absorbed by chlorophyll from sunlight.

*Phototropism*: bending of stems, particularly of indoor plants toward strongest stimulus of light.

*Pistil*: the female organ.

*Pollination*: the transfer of pollen from the anther to the stigma.

*Pot bound*: a condition where a pot-grown plant has filled all of its available soil mass to capacity with root. It is said of some plant subjects to induce flowering, but deterioration will follow if practiced to extreme measures.

*Potting back*: re-potting into a smaller sized pot.

*Potting on*: re-potting into a larger sized pot.

*Potting up*: first potting of a rooted cutting.

*Rubbing out*: removal of unwanted side growths, usually in bud form.

*Second filial generation:* F2 offspring resulting from the crossing of F1 siblings among themselves.

*Sepal*: part of the calyx.

*Siblings*: offspring of same male and female parents.

*Species*: a group whose members have the greatest mutual resemblance.

*Stamen*: the filament and anther in its entirety.

*Stigma*: terminal expansion of the style, surface of the carpel which receives pollen.

*Stopping*: (pinching-out). The removal of a growing tip from stem or branch.

*Striking a cutting*: physical act of inserting a prepared cutting into rooting compost.

*Style*: the stem of the pistil.

*Systemic insecticide*: taken up by the roots and carried into the sap of a plant, thus rendering toxic to sucking insects. Also absorbed by foliage if applied direct.

*Trace element*: (micro nutrient). Required by most plants in minute amounts (at least the elements zinc, boron, manganese, molybdenum and copper) for normal healthy growth. Usually available in most soils, and added to most of todays proprietary brands of fertilisers.

*Tube*: this encloses the pistil and forms the calyx bearer.

*Turgid*: the condition of plant cells after absorption of water to full capacity.

# General Index

# General Index

grooming 103

Haag, Mr 20
Haiti 12
Handley, Mrs E. 18
hardy cultivars 114
Harrison, Mr 16
Hazard & Hazard 20
heteroploids 132
Hodges, Mr 20
Hogg, Mr Thomas 11, 12, 133
Holland, fuchsias in 22
Holmes, Mr R. 18
Henderson, Mr 12, 16
Hispaniola 12
*Hortus Kewensis* 12, 14
hybridising 20, 127, 128, 129

insecticide spray 106, 107; fumigant
    smokes 106, 109; systemic 107
International Registration Authority
    for Fuchsias 20
International Society for Horticult-
    ural Science 20
individual blooms 103
iron 45

Japan 23
Jefferson, Thomas 14
John Innes Institute 35; base fertili-
    ser 36
judging criteria 95; examination 18;
    procedure 95; standard 18

Kew Gardens 13
kieserite 44

Lagan, Dr J.B. 20
Lane, Mr 16
Larwick, Mr A.M. 22
lath house 21; *see also* shade house
leaf hopper 109
Lee, James 12, 13, 14, 15
Lee, Mrs Lilian 21
Lemoine, M. 16
Lindane 108
Linnaeus 11, 13
Los Angeles 21
loam 36, 37
Lye, Mr James 16, 17, 86

MacDougal, Mrs C. and Mr M. 22
magnesium 43, 44
malathion 108
Martin, Mr G. 20
Mendel, Gregor 130; laws of 131
mist spraying 21, 28
molybdenum 46
Munkner, Mr 20
muslin 106, 128
mutation 16
Munz, Professor Phillip 135, 141

National Fuchsia Society 21
Nederlandse Kring van Fuchsia Vrie-
    den 22
Nelson Mr 20

New Zealand, fuchsias in 22
Niederholzer, Mr G. 20, 21
North Island 22
Norway 23
notes 24
*Nova Plantarum Americanum Genera*
    11
nitrogen 44
nutrients 42, 43, 44, 45, 46; defi-
    ciency 45, 47
nylon 73, 128

Parker, Dr Paul 152
peat 37, 38
*Philosophia Botanica* 13
phosphorus 44
photosynthesis 45
phototropism 74, 83, 91
Plumier, Father Carole 11, 133
pollen 127, 128; germination of
    127, 128
polyploid 132
polythene 30, 73
potassium 44, 69
potential hydrogen 38, 39, 42;
    scale 41
pots 34, 94, 113
pot stand 94
potting 32, 34, 35, 75
propagation 23, 25; bench 26, 28,
    105; vegetative 25
pruning 26, 83, 112
pyrethrum 109

reciprocal crosses 128
red spider mite 108
Reedstrom, Mr 20
Rehnelt, M. 16
Reiter, Mr V. 20, 21
Rhodesia, fuchsias in 23
Royal Horticultural Society 13, 18
Rozain-Boucharlat 16
Rumania 23
Rundle, Mr 16
rust 110
Ryle, Dr 18

Sacramento Valley 21
Salisbury 23
Salter, Mr 16
San Diego 21
San Domingo 21
San Francisco 21
Santa Maria 20
Saw-leaved Banksia 13
Schmidt, Mr 20
Schnabel, Mr 20
scorch 32
seed 25; boxes 28, 30; extraction of
    129; sowing 129
shade house 21, 23
shading 31, 32, 106, 130
species 102; types 103
standards 96
Standish, Mr 16
stockinette 94
stock plants 25, 26

166

# Index to Species
# and Cultivars

For the purpose of this index species will be indicated in italics with the genus name omitted.

168